THE MODERN SERVANT LEADER

Emmanuel Randolph Wheagar
The Modern Servant Leader

Published by Spines
ISBN: 979-8-89569-487-9

Spines

THE MODERN SERVANT LEADER

THE PATH TO GLOBAL IMPACT AND LASTING CHANGE

EMMANUEL RANDOLPH WHEAGAR

CONTENTS

To my father, Rev. John N. Wheagar, whose servant leadership, unwavering faith, and love for people profoundly shaped my understanding of true leadership. Your legacy continues to inspire me every day.
To the Almighty God, the leadership teachings of Jesus Christ whose divine guidance and grace have been the cornerstone of my journey and the inspiration behind this work.

And to all the emerging and current leaders who are transforming lives through their leadership, courage, and commitment to making a difference. This book is for you—may it serve as a beacon of purpose and empowerment on your path to greatness.

With deepest gratitude,

Emmanuel

ACKNOWLEDGMENTS

First and foremost, I want to acknowledge the Divine guidance (the Profound leadership teaching of Jesus Christ that has illuminated my path and provided clarity, wisdom, and strength throughout this journey. Without this higher power, the vision behind this book would not have come to fruition.

To my mentors, past and present, who have graciously imparted their knowledge and wisdom, I owe a deep sense of gratitude. Your guidance, challenges, and encouragement have played a critical role in shaping my leadership philosophy. You have shown me what it means to lead with purpose and humility.

I extend my heartfelt appreciation to my family and friends, whose love, support, and critical feedback have been invaluable. You are my anchor. Your honesty in providing constructive assessment pushed me to refine my thoughts and ideas, making this book stronger and irrefutable. Your unwavering belief in me, even during the most challenging moments, kept me moving forward.

Finally, to those who have journeyed alongside me as companions, both personally and professionally, your presence has been a source of inspiration. This book is as much a reflection of your encouragement as it is of my own experiences.

Thank you all for being a part of this meaningful journey.

With deep appreciation,

Emmanuel Randolph Wheagar

ABOUT THE AUTHOR

Emmanuel Randolph Wheagar is a dynamic researcher, leadership and business coach, speaker, entrepreneur, and modern-day leader whose work bridges the timeless wisdom of leadership principles with the demands of the contemporary world. Drawing from the teachings of early leadership pioneers, the moral and ethical guidance found in the Holy Bible, and blending these with cutting-edge strategies, Emmanuel empowers today's leaders to thrive in an ever-evolving, technologically advanced landscape.

His career is marked by a deep commitment to nurturing the next generation of leaders, helping them embrace servant leadership, integrity, emotional intelligence, and purpose-driven decision-making. As a thought leader, Emmanuel emphasizes the importance of combining foundational values with innovation, showing that true leadership is not about power but about the lasting impact one can make by guiding and empowering others.

PREFACE

In an age of rapid change and unprecedented challenges, the need for leaders with purpose has never been more urgent.

When I set out to write *The Modern Servant Leader: The Irrefutable Path to Global Impact and Lasting Change,* my goal was clear: to redefine leadership, moving beyond the conventional models of authority and power to one of service, empathy, and integrity.

Servant leadership isn't new, but its true essence is often misunderstood. Leadership today is too often about control, yet the most transformative leaders serve first, empowering others and inspiring lasting change. This book is born from my personal journey, divine inspiration, and lessons from leaders who have shaped the world. It's for those who wish to lead not just with effectiveness but with deep, lasting fulfillment.

In today's world, leadership must evolve. It's about inspiring trust, fostering collaboration, and creating spaces where people feel seen, heard, and valued. *The Modern Servant Leader* is a guide for leaders at every stage—those seeking to refine their approach and those beginning their journey.

Leadership, when done right, can change lives and reshape the world. Through servant leadership, we have the power to build a future where leadership is not only impactful but profoundly human.

FOREWORD

By Commissioner Dr. Alfred B. Curtis, Jr

In a world where leadership is often defined by titles, power, and hierarchy, it is rare to come across a book that so profoundly redefines what it means to lead. Emmanuel Randolph Wheagar's "The Modern Servant Leader" does exactly that, challenging us to rethink our traditional notions of leadership and guiding us toward a higher purpose—one rooted in service, humility, and empowerment.

In my journey, I've seen countless leaders rise and fall, often by the strength or failure of their ability to connect authentically with those they serve. Leadership, as Emmanuel astutely points out, is not about accumulating power but about distributing it—ensuring that each individual within a team feels valued, heard, and inspired to contribute to something greater than themselves.

As a leadership coach, speaker, serial entrepreneur, and nonprofit executive, Emmanuel has not only transformed organizations but lives. His approach is not theoretical but deeply practical, grounded in his years of hands-on experience leading people from all walks of life. Whether you are guiding a grass-roots organization or a multinational corporation, the principles of servant leadership transcend industry or scale. They speak to the heart of what makes any group of people not only successful but sustainable.

In "The Modern Servant Leader," Emmanuel invites us into a new paradigm—one where leadership is an act of service. This is not just a concept but a lived practice. With compassion and integrity, Emmanuel unpacks the qualities that define a servant leader, from empathy and active listening to fostering an inclusive environment where every individual thrives. His words resonate deeply with those of us who have faced the pressures of leadership and understand that true success is measured not by profits or accolades, but by the impact we have on others.

This book is a roadmap for navigating the complexities of modern leadership. In an age of rapid technological advancement, social unrest, and global uncertainty, the servant leader stands as a beacon of hope and stability. Emmanuel not only provides tools and strategies for implementing servant leadership in your organization but also offers inspiration, reminding us of the profound responsibility we carry as leaders. We are tasked not just with the success of our companies but with the growth and well-being of the people within them.

The depth of Emmanuel's insights is not only timely but urgent. At a time when the world is desperate for leaders who lead with heart, "The Modern Servant Leader" comes as a call to action. It compels us to ask ourselves the difficult questions: Are we leading for the betterment of others? Are we creating spaces where people feel empowered to reach their full potential? Emmanuel's answers to these questions are not just eloquent; they are transformational.

As you turn these pages, prepare to be challenged, inspired, and ultimately changed. "The Modern Servant Leader" is not just a book—it is a movement, a philosophy that has the power to revolutionize how we lead and live.

I am honored to write this foreword, not only because I believe in the principles Emmanuel so passionately advocates but because I know, from my own experiences in leadership, that his message is one the world desperately needs. Emmanuel is the embodiment of the modern servant leader, and this book is his gift to us all. Take his wisdom, apply it, and watch how your leadership—and your life—are transformed.

Dr. Alfred B. Curtis, Jr.

CEO - A. Boima Curtis & Associates, LLC

Former Commissioner for Youth and Community Development - New York City

Former CEO – United Nations Development Corporation

INTRODUCTION

The Modern Servant Leader

With over two decades of experience in leadership roles and having studied the strategies of more than 100 great leaders, I've come to a powerful realization: in today's fast-paced, interconnected world, leadership must undergo a radical transformation. To inspire, lead, and thrive in this new era, leaders must embrace bold new approaches that challenge traditional norms and adapt to an ever-evolving influence of leadership in action.

Managing outcomes is no longer enough—today's leaders must nurture relationships, inspire collaboration, and drive innovation. This book introduces servant leadership as a transformative model for modern leaders, whether you're an entrepreneur, pastor, CEO, or director. Rooted in timeless principles, it emphasizes humility, empathy, and empowering others. In a world shaped by global conflicts, climate change, and rapid technological advancements, servant leadership provides the wisdom and practical tools to not only survive but thrive.

The foundation of servant leadership is the belief that true greatness lies in serving others, as stated in Matthew 23:11: "The greatest among you will be your servant." This book challenges traditional leadership models focused on control, offering instead a transformative approach that empowers others. Servant leaders inspire innovation and trust by leading from behind, fostering a culture of collaboration and shared vision. Whether managing a small team or leading a global organization, this book provides actionable insights for cultivating a team's strengths, building trust, and leading with courage, vulnerability, and unwavering values.

Lastly, **sustaining impact and legacy** is at the core of servant leadership. Great leaders do more than achieve short-term success; they create lasting change by mentoring others and empowering them to take ownership of their roles. As the Bible teaches in Matthew 20:26-28, leadership is about serving others, not seeking personal gain. This section will guide you in building a leadership legacy that extends beyond your tenure, turning followers into future leaders who can carry your vision forward.

Ultimately, this book is an invitation to redefine leadership—not just for yourself, but for the communities and organizations you serve. Through the principles of servant leadership, you'll learn to lead with purpose, empathy, and courage, creating a lasting, positive impact on those around you. Let this guide serve as a tool to help you navigate the challenges of today's world and inspire you to lead with a servant's heart.

LEADING FROM BEHIND

The Power of Servant Leadership

At first glance, "leading from behind" may seem counterintuitive —aren't leaders meant to guide from the front? Traditional leadership often ties authority to dominance and control, yet this model can exhaust leaders and confine followers to passive roles.

In Mark 10:42-44 and Matthew 20:25-28, Jesus redefines leadership: *"Whoever would be great among you must be your servant."* True leadership prioritizes humility, service, and the well-being of others, as seen in Jesus' example of serving rather than being served. Similarly, *John 10:11* reminds us of the Good Shepherd, who lays down His life for His sheep, emphasizing leadership as an act of selfless care and empowerment.

Nelson Mandela echoed this approach, describing leadership as shepherding—guiding from behind while enabling others to thrive. This quiet strength inspires teams to greatness without seeking the spotlight. Imagine the transformation if every leader embraced this philosophy, valuing their teams with gratitude and empowering them to shine

Barack Obama's Strategy: Trusting the Team and Leading from Behind

Barack Obama's leadership exemplified trust and empowerment, fostering collaboration and driving significant achievements. During the 2009 economic crisis, he relied on experts like Treasury Secretary Timothy Geithner and NEC Director Larry Summers to implement the $787 billion American Recovery and Reinvestment Act. This trust-based approach stabilized the economy, saved over 1.5 million jobs, and reduced unemployment to below 5% by 2016.

Obama's belief in collective effort reflects the Parable of the Talents (Matthew 25:14-30), where trust in others' abilities leads to growth and success. As the master praised his servants for wisely using their talents, Obama empowered his team to act decisively. This approach also aligns with Proverbs 3:5-6: "Trust in the Lord with all your heart and lean not on your own understanding."

By delegating authority and encouraging initiative, Obama demonstrated that effective leadership lies in empowering others, fostering collaboration, and achieving sustainable success. His model serves as a blueprint for leaders seeking to inspire trust and drive meaningful change.

The Superpower of Leading from Behind

True leadership isn't about commanding from the front—it's about empowering from behind. This transformative style, known as servant leadership, builds trust, fosters innovation, and unites teams by elevating every voice. It's leadership rooted in humility and strength, unlocking the hidden potential within others to create lasting success.

Research from the *Journal of Business Ethics* shows servant-led teams achieve 12% higher performance and 33% greater employee engagement, proving that empowering others isn't just a moral choice—it's a strategic advantage. Ed Catmull, co-founder of Pixar, exemplified this by trusting his team to push creative boundaries. That trust gave the world groundbreaking films like *Toy Story* and *Inside Out* while fostering a culture of collaboration and excellence.

As Michelle Obama put it, *"People who are truly strong lift others up. People who are truly powerful bring others together."* Leading from behind is transformative. It shifts the focus from dominance to empowerment, creating leaders who inspire loyalty, spark innovation, and prevent burnout.

Nelson Mandela captured this philosophy perfectly: *"It is better to lead from behind and to put others in front, especially when you celebrate victory. You only take the front line when there is danger."* By guiding others to shine, leaders create a culture where growth and leadership thrive at every level.

Simon Sinek reminds us: *"Leadership is not about being in charge. It's about taking care of those in your charge."* Leading from behind isn't a weakness—it's the ultimate strength. It's a call to elevate, inspire, and build a legacy of trust and shared success.

The Paradox of External Leadership

Many leaders fail to build other leaders, this is precisely why so many companies resort to hiring CEOs from outside their own organizations. How does it make sense that an organization, often decades old, cannot find a single leader within its ranks capable of stepping up?

I am not suggesting that leading from behind means abdicating responsibility or passively allowing others to dictate direction. To do so would be a recipe for disaster. True leadership doesn't involve stepping back and folding your arms; it involves empowering others while maintaining a firm grip on your core values and executive responsibilities.

The servant leader empowers successors from within, instilling the company's culture, values, and vision. When challenges arise, the team collaborates to find solutions. However, when internal leadership is absent, an outsider may be hired, sometimes with undesired results.

A classic example: The downfall of J.C. Penney under CEO Ron Johnson serves as a painful reminder. His outsider perspective ignored the company's established culture, resulting in a rapid loss of customers and trust, and continues to struggle.

As John Maxwell wisely said, *"A leader is one who knows the way, goes the way, and shows the way."* Leadership is about guiding with empathy and understanding, not simply asserting control.

Stepping Back: The Power of Servant Leadership

Imagine a leader who steps back—not out of hesitation, but with intention—to unlock the strengths and potential of every team member. This is servant leadership, a transformative approach where guiding others to succeed takes precedence over commanding control. It's leadership rooted in service, trust, and collaboration, fostering a culture where innovation and growth thrive.

As Robert K. Greenleaf, the father of servant leadership, profoundly stated, *"The servant-leader is servant first."* This philosophy redefines leadership as an act of humility and empowerment, inspiring teams to reach extraordinary heights.

Consider Southwest Airlines under Herb Kelleher's leadership. By prioritizing employee well-being and growth, Kelleher fostered a culture of empowerment that fueled extraordinary success. From 1990 to 2000, Southwest's stock price skyrocketed by 1,000%, and by 2023, it remained a top airline with annual revenue exceeding $27 billion. This enduring success proves that servant leadership isn't just a noble concept—it's a powerful, sustainable strategy.

Southwest's journey underscores a vital truth: when leaders step back to elevate others, they create lasting impact—building organizations that thrive on trust, collaboration, and shared purpose.

Nurturing Future Leaders: A Rarity in Modern Leadership

The Modern Servant leadership concept emphasizes that a true leader cares for their team's well-being, prioritizes their growth, and stands by them during challenges. A "Good Shepherd" leader is committed, supportive, and serves their people selflessly—qualities that foster trust, loyalty, and team success.

*In **John 10:11-15**, Jesus describes himself as the "Good Shepherd", a servant leader who cares deeply for his flock, even to the point of sacrificing his life for them.*

A good leader does not walk ahead of his staff demanding compliance from a position of superiority. Instead, he stays behind, observing with care and compassion, nurturing and ensuring no one is left behind. Leading from behind gives leaders the ability to assess their team holistically—identifying the weak, the strong, the fast, the sick, and the exceptionally gifted. It's a leadership approach that fosters growth and development rather than fear and dependency. Leadership should liberate, not intimidate.

As Dr. Myles Munroe famously said, *"Trapped in every follower is a leader."* The role of a leader is to unlock that leadership potential, not to suppress it.

Fear-Based Leadership: A Toxic Cycle

Are your followers merely parasites, crippled by fear, following your lead because they have no other choice? Do they tremble at your presence, only to feel relieved and carefree the moment you're out of sight? This fear-driven dynamic is a hallmark of toxic leadership, where followers obey out of anxiety rather than respect.

Fear-based leadership is a harmful approach that undermines both employees and organizations. It erodes morale and trust, creating a toxic environment where employees feel unsupported and disengaged. When fear prevails, creativity and collaboration are stifled, as individuals become hesitant to take risks or share new ideas.

Constant stress and anxiety lead to burnout, absenteeism, and a decline in overall well-being. Productivity suffers, as fear distracts and demotivates. Ultimately, this leadership style damages the very culture and growth an organization needs to thrive.

The Bible also speaks to the destructive nature of fear: *"For God gave us a spirit not of fear but of power and love and self-control"* (2 Timothy 1:7). True leadership should inspire, empower, and build trust, not instill fear.

Fear-based leadership will keep your businesses, churches, or organizations, or governments stagnated and mediocre. Fear based leadership will employ nepotism over qualified candidates for a succession or key positions.

The Servant Leader is a Cheerleader

A servant leader acts as a cheerleader, encouraging and building morale, and reports to their followers toward success. According to a report by the *Harvard Business Review*, the leaders who will thrive in the coming decade will be those who embrace the practice of leading from behind. They cheer their teams on by coaching, motivating, inspiring, and celebrating both small victories and major accomplishments.

Rather than seeking personal accolades, the servant leader finds joy in the success of others. They uplift their team, acting like a tailwind that boosts the morale and energy of the people they lead. The servant leader taps into the power of collective genius, understanding that greatness comes not from individual brilliance but from the strength of a united, empowered group.

A Legacy of Empowerment - The Servant Leader's Lasting Impact

A true servant leader doesn't seek the spotlight but finds fulfillment in empowering others. By creating opportunities for their team to step up—whether leading a presentation or representing the organization at critical meetings—they forge a legacy of resilience and shared success. This approach ensures that the organization's strength is rooted not in a single leader but in a well-equipped, empowered team.

According to a recent Gallup study, teams with leaders who prioritize employee development see a 24% increase in productivity and 21% greater profitability, underscoring the tangible benefits of empowerment-based leadership. "A good leader inspires people to have confidence in the leader; a great leader inspires people to have confidence in themselves," noted Eleanor Roosevelt—a timeless principle that speaks to the heart of servant leadership.

The success of **The Container Store** is a compelling case in point. Founded on servant leadership principles, the company has consistently been named one of Fortune's "100 Best Companies to Work For" due to its focus on employee empowerment. In 2023, their employee satisfaction rate was over 90%, reflecting a high-trust environment that leads to lower turnover and improved customer experience.

As Proverbs 11:14 states, "Where there is no guidance, a people fall, but in an abundance of counselors there is safety." Servant leaders embody this wisdom, investing in others to create a sustainable, thriving legacy beyond themselves.

The Servant Leader Shares Power and Gains Influence

It is an irony of leadership that the more power you give, the more powerful you become. Only the wise will understand this concept. True servant leaders understand that real strength is not about holding onto control but about sharing it. Forbes Magazine captured this in their article, *"In Troubled Times, President Obama Continues to Lead from Behind"*, highlighting how Barack Obama exemplified this leadership style during his presidency. Richard Miniter, New York Times bestselling author and former Wall Street Journal writer, wrote a compelling analysis of how Obama's behind-the-scenes leadership defied expectations yet drove profound success.

To his critics on the Republican right, Obama was a master strategist operating from the shadows, while to his supporters, he was the champion who fought for justice and equality. But both sides agreed on one thing: Obama was a servant leader who led from behind, empowering his cabinet and staff to flourish. This leadership style wasn't about him—it was about unlocking the potential of the team around him.

When people feel trusted, they perform beyond expectations. This principle is at the heart of leading from behind.

Leading the Modern Workforce

In today's workforce, people are no longer driven solely by salary or job security. Employees, church workers, volunteers, contractors, and even government officials are increasingly motivated by the desire to be heard, to find meaning, and to make a tangible difference. The servant leader recognizes this shift and crafts an environment where every effort is acknowledged every voice is valued, and every achievement is celebrated. This nurturing culture doesn't merely retain talent—it fosters deep loyalty as individuals feel seen and appreciated not for rewards, but for their intrinsic contributions.

The leaders who will inspire the workforce of the 21st century is not those who cling to power or ego, but those who willingly share their influence.

Studies from the *Harvard Business Review* show that organizations led with empathy and collaboration experience a 22% increase in overall employee satisfaction and a marked improvement in team resilience. The modern servant leader, like Ardern, acts as a guide, a coach, and a champion of collective success—understanding that when their followers are uplifted, so too is the entire organization.

The Servant Leader Understands the Deep Human Need for Validation

But why does this matter so much? Because deep down, each of us desires to be seen and valued—not just for our productivity, but for who we are. As Michelle Obama insightfully remarked, "People who are truly strong lift others up. People who are truly powerful bring others together". Servant leaders tap into this universal need for belonging, contribution, and growth. They create space for others to step into their full potential. This kind of leadership transforms lives.

Human beings have a fundamental need for validation, which is crucial for emotional well-being, self-esteem, and mental health. Recent studies confirm the biological and psychological importance of validation.

A 2023 study published in *Frontiers in Psychology* found that social validation reduces stress, with individuals receiving positive feedback showing lower cortisol levels. Similarly, a 2020 study in *Psychological Science* revealed that recognition enhances self-esteem and motivation, creating a positive feedback loop that boosts performance.

Real-world examples highlight the impact of validation. For instance, Google's recognition programs contribute to high employee satisfaction, with 87% of employees feeling valued in 2023, contributing to innovation and success. In education, a 2022 study found that students who received regular validation from teachers were 30% more likely to engage and perform better academically.

However, excessive reliance on social media validation can be harmful. A 2021 study from the University of Pennsylvania found that constant virtual feedback can lead to anxiety and depression, especially in adolescents.

Essentially, to the servant leader, staff and employee validation is essential for well-being and success, and its impact spans from workplaces to classrooms and beyond. Understanding this need can lead to stronger relationships, improved performance, and better mental health.

The Modern Leadership Landscape

As Linda Hill from the Harvard Business Review notes, today's world demands leaders who can collaborate and build strong, interdependent teams. The era of the lone hero leader is fading. In the 21st century, leadership is about lifting others, and in doing so, both the leaders and their teams grow.

The Irony of Empowerment

The truth is, that people don't want to work for leaders who are obsessed with power. They want to be part of something bigger than themselves. They want to belong to a team where their contributions matter. When you lead from behind, you give them that gift. Ironically, the more you empower others, the stronger you become. When people feel trusted, they don't just meet expectations—they exceed them. They become more loyal, more dedicated, and more willing to go the extra mile.

The Future of Leadership: The Transformative Power of Leading from Behind

The leaders who will shape the future are those who understand a profound truth: true leadership is found in service. As Matthew 20:26 says, "But among you it will be different. Whoever wants to be a leader among you must be your servant." This timeless wisdom reminds us that authentic leadership isn't about dominance but about empowering others.

Real power arises not from control but from connection. Modern servant leaders don't seek authority to wield power; they seek it to create spaces where people feel valued, heard, and inspired. As Nelson Mandela said, "It is better to lead from behind and to put others in front, especially when you celebrate victory when nice things occur. You take the front line when there is danger. Then people will appreciate your leadership."

In today's world, a successful organization is not built by the leader alone, but by the community that the leader cultivates. When leaders prioritize the well-being, growth, and voice of their people, they create an environment where innovation thrives, collaboration deepens, and purpose drives every action.

Through this collective strength, organizations move beyond transient success to build legacies that last.

A Quiet Revolution in Leadership

Leading from behind is not a retreat but a profound leap forward. This approach redefines the role of a leader, shifting the spotlight from individual achievement to the collective brilliance of the team. It represents a quiet revolution, transcending traditional models of command and control, and embracing a dynamic, empowering way of guiding others.

Research supports the power of this approach. A study published in *The Leadership Quarterly* found that servant leadership significantly improves employee engagement and organizational performance. Teams led by servant leaders reported a 23% increase in commitment and a 17% rise in performance metrics compared to teams under traditional leadership models. This study demonstrates how servant leadership not only fosters individual well-being but also enhances overall productivity and success.

As Napoleon Hill once said, "It is literally true that you can succeed best and quickest by helping others to succeed." This insight encapsulates the essence of servant leadership, where the focus is on elevating others rather than asserting authority. By prioritizing the growth and empowerment of the team, leaders create environments where creativity, loyalty, and excellence naturally flourish, transforming organizations from within.

This quiet revolution suggests that lasting success is rooted in shared purpose and mutual support, building resilient teams capable of extraordinary achievements. Through collective strength, servant leaders drive real progress—leaving behind not just successful outcomes, but a legacy of trust, collaboration, and enduring impact.

Inspiring Rather Than Commanding

Imagine a world where leadership is defined not by how loudly one can command but by how deeply one can inspire. This is the essence of leading from behind—a call to create environments where every voice is heard, every talent is nurtured, and every individual is empowered to shine. It's about cultivating a culture of trust, respect, and collaboration, where the leader's greatest strength lies in their ability to create space for others to excel.

In today's leadership landscape, figures like Satya Nadella, CEO of Microsoft, exemplify this approach. Under his guidance, Microsoft transformed from a culture of competition to one of collaboration, innovation, and empathy. Nadella, in his book *Hit Refresh,* emphasized the importance of empathy in leadership, saying, "Leadership is not about being in charge. It's about taking care of those in your charge." Research supports this idea: a study from the Center for Creative Leadership found that empathy is a core competency for effective leadership, with leaders who demonstrate empathy fostering stronger team performance, higher morale, and lower turnover.

The Bible echoes this approach to leadership in Philippians 2:3-4, which says, "Do nothing from selfish ambition or conceit, but in humility count others more significant than yourselves. Let each of you look not only to his own interests but also to the interests of others." This verse reflects the heart of servant leadership, where leaders prioritize the growth and well-being of others, lifting them up to reach their potential. In this way, leadership becomes not a position of authority but a commitment to empower and support others.

Amplifying Your Staff's Capabilities

As you step into your leadership role, remember that *leading from behind* is not about relinquishing control; it's about magnifying the potential and aspirations of those around you. This leadership style emphasizes empowerment and shared purpose, which, as recent studies show, drive both individual and organizational success. For example, Gallup reports that companies with highly engaged employees outperform their competitors by 147% in earnings per share, highlighting the power of an empowered workforce to transform organizational outcomes.

Howard Schultz, the visionary behind Starbucks, exemplified this principle, famously saying, "When you're surrounded by people who share a passionate commitment around a common purpose, anything is possible." His servant leadership approach, which emphasizes the growth and well-being of others, propelled Starbucks into a globally respected brand. By calling his employees "partners" and investing in a positive, inclusive company culture, Schultz cultivated trust and loyalty, enabling employees to contribute to a common vision with passion and purpose.

Research supports this approach. A Deloitte study reveals that 94% of executives and 88% of employees believe that a distinct workplace culture is vital to business success. Moreover, organizations prioritizing trust and respect often see an increase in innovation and productivity, with these factors contributing to up to a 50% increase in employee performance. Leaders who focus on these values foster a deep sense of belonging, purpose, and ownership among their teams, sparking innovation and creativity.

This perspective aligns with the wisdom in *Proverbs 27:17*, which states, "As iron sharpens iron, so one person sharpens another." By elevating others, leaders create a cycle of mutual growth, where individuals are inspired to strive not only for their own success but for the collective vision. In doing so, they fulfill a calling that transcends personal ambition, building a legacy of resilience, collaboration, and shared achievement.

Conclusion: The Lasting Power of Leading from Behind

As this chapter closes, take with you the transformative wisdom of leading from behind. This leadership style—centered on empowering others—reveals that true greatness lies in fostering talent, embracing collaboration, and creating a legacy that endures long after the spotlight fades.

Modern leaders like Nelson Mandela, Jacinda Ardern, and Satya Nadella exemplify this approach, proving that influence comes not from commanding attention but from elevating others. The results speak for themselves: organizations with inclusive cultures are six times more likely to innovate and twice as likely to meet financial goals, according to McKinsey.

To apply this wisdom:

- **Invest in Growth**: Provide opportunities for learning—94% of employees say they'd stay longer with employers who do (LinkedIn).
- **Build Trust**: Foster accountability and mutual respect; trust-driven workplaces boost engagement by 74% (PwC).
- **Lead with Humility**: Model patience and openness—engaged teams increase by 23% under humble leaders (Harvard Business Review).

As Albert Schweitzer observed, *"The only ones among you who will be really happy are those who will have sought and found how to serve.*" By leading from behind, you inspire collective greatness, shaping a resilient, inclusive future that transcends any single achievement.

THE POWER OF HUMILITY

In times of global uncertainty, humility stands as a defining strength of leadership—uniting people, inspiring empathy, and transforming challenges into opportunities. Far from weakness, humility fosters trust, bridges divide, and cultivates collaboration. As Rabindranath Tagore observed, *"We come nearest to the great when we are great in humility."*

Leaders like Warren Buffett and Mary Barra demonstrate how humility drives resilience and innovation, while bold figures like Donald Trump appeal to those seeking decisive action. Yet, history proves that humility sustains true leadership, empowering others through compassion and connection.

The Essence of Humility in Leadership

Humility is not about thinking less of oneself but thinking of oneself less. As C.S. Lewis wisely said, *"True humility fosters genuine connection and leadership."* It is the courage to listen, the grace to admit flaws, and the strength to prioritize others.

In a world increasingly shaped by rapid technological shifts and social challenges, humility remains vital. Research shows that

58% of employees prefer humble, approachable leaders, while servant leadership—marked by humility, empathy, and collaboration—boosts engagement by 30% and productivity by 23%.

Biblical wisdom underscores humility's power: *"Do nothing out of selfish ambition... Rather, in humility, value others above yourselves"* (Philippians 2:3-4). This principle of servant leadership creates environments where innovation thrives and collective success is achieved.

Leaders Who Exemplify Humility

Tim Cook's quiet leadership at Apple prioritizes listening, empathy, and team recognition, fostering a culture of innovation. Malala Yousafzai, despite her global acclaim, shares the spotlight, proving that true leadership uplifts others.

Conversely, Elon Musk's bold vision sometimes lacks the humility needed for collaboration, underscoring that even brilliance needs balance. Leaders who embrace humility build trust and inspire loyalty—traits Gen Z values in inclusive, collaborative spaces.

The Transformative Power of Humility

Rick Warren captures humility's essence: *"Humility is not denying your strengths but being honest about your weaknesses."* It is the cornerstone of transformative leadership, driving meaningful change by inspiring collective effort.

In a world craving connection, humility in leadership creates an enduring impact, shaping organizations and communities to thrive. True greatness lies not in commanding others but in empowering them to succeed.

The Humble Trailblazers: Leaders Who Transform Through Humility

In today's fast-paced world, humility in leadership is not merely a virtue—it's a catalyst for trust, collaboration, and innovation. By recognizing their flaws, uplifting others, and leading with empathy, humble leaders create environments where teams thrive and achieve extraordinary results.

1. Tim Cook – Apple

Tim Cook's inclusive leadership style emphasizes collaboration and team recognition. Under his guidance since 2011, Apple became the first company to hit a $2 trillion valuation. Cook's preference for a low-profile, team-first approach fosters innovation and high employee engagement.

- **Impact**: Harvard Business Review found companies with humble leaders see a 25% increase in employee engagement. By 2023, Apple's revenue exceeded $365 billion.

2. Satya Nadella – Microsoft

Satya Nadella's humility transformed Microsoft's culture into one of collaboration and growth. By embracing empathy and a growth mindset, he led the company to unprecedented success.

- **Impact**: Microsoft's market value surged from $300 billion in 2014 to over $2.5 trillion in 2023. Deloitte reports that servant leadership boosts innovation by 40%.

3. Malala Yousafzai – Malala Fund

Despite global recognition, Malala Yousafzai remains grounded, sharing credit with her team. Her humility amplifies her message of advocating for girls' education worldwide.

- **Impact**: The Malala Fund has reached over 100 million girls in 20 countries. McKinsey found leaders prioritizing social causes increase public trust by 25%.

4. Howard Schultz – Starbucks

Howard Schultz built Starbucks into a global brand by focusing on employee well-being and inclusivity. His servant leadership approach prioritized fair wages and health benefits, creating a supportive culture.

- **Impact**: Starbucks' annual revenues exceeded $30 billion. Gallup found companies with humble leaders have 18% higher employee retention and satisfaction.

5. Abigail Johnson – Fidelity Investments

Abigail Johnson's transparent and approachable leadership at Fidelity emphasizes collaboration and long-term growth.

- **Impact**: Fidelity's assets under management grew from $2 trillion to $4.5 trillion under her leadership. Gallup links humble leadership to 25% higher revenue growth.

Humble leaders transform challenges into opportunities, building cultures of trust and innovation that drive sustained success. These trailblazers prove that humility isn't just admirable—it's essential for impactful leadership.

The Impact of Humility in Leadership

Humility is a transformative leadership trait with proven benefits across industries. Leaders who prioritize humility are more likely to:

- **Foster Innovation**: Inclusive cultures that encourage collaboration and creativity.
- **Build Loyal Teams**: Higher retention rates and stronger team cohesion.
- **Drive Financial Growth**: Organizations led by humble leaders see revenue growth rates up to 25% higher.
- **Cultivate Trust**: Humble leaders are viewed as more empathetic and approachable, creating high-performing teams.

Trailblazers like Tim Cook at Apple, Satya Nadella at Microsoft, and Howard Schultz at Starbucks demonstrate that humility fuels long-term success. These leaders have shown that putting others first sparks innovation builds trust, and drives enduring impact.

As Mahatma Gandhi aptly said, *"The best way to find yourself is to lose yourself in the service of others."* Humility is not a weakness but a force that inspires, empowers, and transforms.

Leading with Humility: The Cornerstone of Effective Leadership

Humility defines great leadership. It's about guiding with empathy, respect, and collaboration rather than control. Leaders like Dr. Alfred B. Curtis, former Commissioner of New York City's Department of Youth and Community Development, embodied this by treating everyone with respect and staying behind to clean up after events—showing that leadership is service, not status.

As the Dalai Lama said, *"Humility is the solid foundation of all virtues."*

The Bible echoes this truth: *"But he that is greatest among you shall be your servant. And whosoever shall exalt himself shall be abased, and he that shall humble himself shall be exalted."* (Matthew 23:11-12, KJV)

Humble leaders seek input, celebrate small victories, and own their mistakes, creating a culture where everyone feels valued, heard, and inspired. This collaborative spirit drives innovation and collective success, proving that humility isn't a weakness but a transformative strength.

Examples of Humble Leadership

Howard Schultz – Starbucks

Howard Schultz, former CEO of Starbucks, exemplified humility by prioritizing respect and listening to employees. He fostered a supportive culture, empowering staff to thrive and deliver exceptional customer experiences. Schultz's leadership transformed Starbucks from a single coffee shop into a global powerhouse, generating over $30 billion in annual revenue. Research by Gallup confirms that companies with humble leaders see a 25% boost in employee engagement, driving productivity and success.

Joe Biden – U.S. Presidency

President Joe Biden exemplifies humility through his inclusive leadership and trust in others. By entrusting Kamala Harris with significant responsibilities during his presidency, Biden has amplified diverse voices and empowered future leadership.

In a historic move, Biden announced he would step back, turning over his second presidential campaign to Vice President Harris, making her the Democratic front-runner for the 2024 presidential elections and the party's standard-bearer. This decision underscores his commitment to unity, progress, and fostering new leadership.

As Proverbs 18:12 (KJV) states: "Before destruction the heart of man is haughty, and before honor is humility." Biden's actions reflect this truth, rooted in humility and a vision for the future.

Humble leaders like Schultz and Biden prove that humility fosters trust, loyalty, and meaningful impact, reminding us that true leadership lies in service and empowerment.

The Power of Humble Leadership

The Bible teaches that humility is the cornerstone of great leadership. As Philippians 2:3-4 (KJV) reminds us: *"Let nothing be done through strife or vainglory, but in lowliness of mind let each esteem other better than themselves. Look not every man on his own things, but every man also on the things of others."* Humble leaders prioritize the well-being of others, fostering trust, respect, and shared success.

Impact and Research Findings

Recent studies underscore the transformative impact of humility in leadership:

- A Harvard Business Review study found that humble leaders enhance employee retention by 18% and boost collaboration and creativity by 20%.
- Deloitte reports that companies with humble leaders achieve 30% greater long-term success and 40% higher innovation rates.

A Real-Life Example: Satya Nadella – Microsoft

Satya Nadella, CEO of Microsoft, transformed the company's culture with his humble leadership. Taking the helm in 2014, Nadella focused on listening, learning, and encouraging collaboration. He shifted Microsoft's culture from competition to teamwork, enabling remarkable innovation and growth. Under his leadership, Microsoft's market value soared from $300 billion to over $2.5 trillion by 2023. Nadella's humility and empathy created a workplace where employees felt valued, driving unprecedented success.

A Timeless Truth

Humility is not weakness but strength under control. As leadership expert John C. Maxwell says: *"A leader is one who knows the way, goes the way, and shows the way."* Through humility, leaders like Nadella and others inspire and empower, proving that the path to greatness is paved with service and selflessness.

The ERW Humility Skill: Best-Practice Guide to Transformative Servant Leadership

The ERW Humility Skill is not just a framework—it's a revolutionary approach that redefines leadership for the modern era. In a world where trust is fragile, and collaboration is the key to success, humility has emerged as a superpower for leaders who aspire to foster a thriving, inclusive, and high-performing culture. With this skill, leaders learn to reflect on their behaviors, adapt to challenges, and cultivate environments where their teams feel valued, heard, and motivated. The result? Increased productivity, stronger relationships, and a profound sense of purpose.

Rooted in modern research and time-tested leadership principles, the ERW Humility Scale equips leaders to confront the complexities of leadership with grace and authenticity. This guide is for leaders who understand that true strength lies not in dominance, but in service, humility, and the empowerment of others.

1. **Speak Less, Act More**

The principle: Humble leaders prioritize action over rhetoric. Instead of dominating discussions, they lead by example, showing their values through deeds rather than words.

Modern Data: According to a 2020 study by the Center for Leadership Studies, leaders who actively listen and take initiative see a 15% increase in team engagement and a 20% rise in productivity.

Example: Satya Nadella, CEO of Microsoft (appointed in 2014), transformed the company by focusing on listening to his employees and fostering a culture of innovation. His leadership led to a 30% increase in stock value by 2019, driven by his emphasis on action over talk.

Emotion: Leaders who speak less and act more create an atmosphere of trust. This approach reminds teams that their leader's commitment is genuine and that actions truly reflect values.

2. **Praise Small Achievements**

The principle: Recognizing even the smallest wins encourages a culture of appreciation. Humble leaders celebrate progress, no matter how minor, reinforcing a positive work environment.

Modern Data: Gallup's 2019 report found that employees who receive regular praise are 3.5 times more likely to be engaged and 4 times more likely to remain with their company.

Example: At Zappos, Tony Hsieh famously emphasized the importance of celebrating all achievements, no matter how small, which helped the company become one of the most loved brands in the retail industry.

Emotion: By celebrating small wins, leaders make individuals feel valued and motivated, cultivating an environment where optimism and morale flourish.

3. **Motivate and Uplift Others**

The principle: Humble leaders focus on uplifting others, helping their team members believe in themselves and reach their full potential.

Modern Data: A 2017 study by the Harvard Business Review revealed that leaders who empower their teams create a 33% increase in job satisfaction and 27% higher employee retention rates.

Example: a globally admired leader, Oprah Winfrey has built an empire by empowering others. She fosters the belief in her employees, helping them realize their potential and shine in their roles.

Emotion: Humble leaders ignite a sense of possibility within their teams. By motivating others, they create a ripple effect of positivity that elevates the collective spirit.

4. **Lead by Serving**

The principle: Humble leaders prioritize the needs of their teams. They demonstrate their commitment by taking on tasks that support the group's success.

Modern Data: Research by the Greenleaf Center for Servant Leadership shows that servant leadership leads to a 25% increase in team collaboration and a 20% increase in trust across all levels of an organization.

Example: Jeff Bezos's leadership at Amazon, while controversial in its early years, shifted in the 2010s toward a servant-leader model, focusing on empowering employees. Amazon's annual revenue increased from $61 billion in 2012 to $469 billion by 2021.

Emotion: Leading by serving builds mutual respect and loyalty. Teams feel empowered when they know their leader prioritizes their success over personal gain.

5. **Mentor, Don't Compete**

The principle: Humble leaders see their role as mentors, not competitors. They share their knowledge freely, guiding others to success without feeling threatened by their growth.

Modern Data: According to a study by the Center for Creative Leadership, leaders who mentor their employees are 30% more likely to inspire innovation within their teams.

Example: Google's leadership, especially under founders Larry Page and Sergey Brin, has always emphasized mentorship. They provide access to leadership development programs and encourage a non-competitive atmosphere where employees can thrive.

Emotion: Leaders who embrace mentoring create a deep sense of gratitude and loyalty within their teams. When employees feel supported in their growth, they are more likely to invest their best efforts into the organization.

6. **Admit Mistakes**

The principle: Humble leaders show vulnerability by admitting when they are wrong. This builds trust and reinforces the idea that mistakes are part of growth.

Modern Data: A 2018 study by the Journal of Business and Psychology found that employees who observe their leaders admitting mistakes are 40% more likely to embrace a culture of feedback and continuous improvement.

Example: When Elon Musk publicly acknowledged errors in Tesla's production processes, he not only gained respect but also engaged his team in solving complex issues, improving efficiency by 15% in 2020.

Emotion: Admitting mistakes humanizes leaders, making them more relatable and trustworthy. This honesty fosters a culture where learning from failures is seen as an opportunity rather than a setback.

7. **Use a Team Approach**

The principle: Humble leaders prioritize collaboration over hierarchy. They value the input of every team member, creating a sense of ownership in shared goals.

Modern Data: Google's Project Aristotle (2012) found that the most successful teams were those with a high level of psychological safety, where leaders actively foster collaboration and respect diverse opinions.

Example: Salesforce CEO Marc Benioff advocates for the "Ohana culture," where every employee is treated as family. This inclusive approach has made Salesforce one of the most innovative and socially responsible companies of the 21st century.

Emotion: When leaders create an environment of psychological safety, they cultivate a sense of belonging, where individuals feel their voices matter and their contributions are valued.

8. **Reprimand Without Condescension**

The principle: Humble leaders address performance issues respectfully, with a focus on growth rather than punishment.

Modern Data: Research shows that constructive feedback leads to a 40% higher improvement in performance compared to punitive measures.

Example: At Pixar, leaders emphasize constructive feedback through regular "notes" sessions where everyone, including top executives, can offer suggestions. This culture of open feedback has led to consistently successful movies, such as *Toy Story 3* (2010), which grossed over $1 billion globally.

Emotion: Addressing mistakes with respect and care encourages openness and reduces anxiety, ensuring that team members are empowered to improve rather than feeling defeated.

9. **Engage with All Staff Levels**

The principle: Humble leaders make an effort to engage with employees at all levels, fostering a culture of inclusivity and respect.

Modern Data: A 2016 study by Gallup found that employees who engage with their leaders at all levels are 15% more productive and 25% more likely to remain with the company.

Example: Richard Branson of Virgin Group is known for his direct engagement with employees, from front-line workers to executives. This approach has helped Virgin maintain a unique culture that values every employee's input.

Emotion: Engaging with all staff levels makes individuals feel heard and respected, which strengthens their emotional commitment to the team and company.

10. **Participate in Community Projects**

The principle: Humble leaders recognize the importance of giving back and engage in community projects that align with their values.

Modern Data: Companies with leaders who participate in social initiatives experience a 20% increase in brand loyalty and a 25% increase in employee satisfaction.

Example: Ben & Jerry's, under the leadership of Ben Cohen and Jerry Greenfield, has consistently engaged in environmental and social justice projects. Their leadership in these areas has enhanced the brand's global reputation and built deep connections with their customer base.

Emotion: Community involvement instills a sense of pride and shared purpose, where employees and leaders alike feel connected to something greater than themselves.

11. **Wear a Genuine Smile**

The principle: Humble leaders greet others with warmth and openness, creating an inviting atmosphere that encourages trust and collaboration.

Modern Data: A 2019 study in *The Journal of Applied Psychology* found that leaders who demonstrate warmth increase team cooperation by 33%, fostering an environment of openness and trust.

Example: When Bill Gates interacts with his team, his genuine warmth and approachable demeanor make people feel at ease, allowing them to share ideas and collaborate openly.

Emotion: A smile can convey trust, warmth, and optimism. It has the power to disarm tension and create a sense of safety, making team members feel heard and respected.

The Quiet Strength of Humility: A Transformative Force in Leadership

Humility, often seen as a quiet virtue, is the bedrock of transformative leadership. As Ernest Hemingway aptly said, *"True nobility is being superior to your former self."* Humble leaders focus not on self-promotion but on fostering collaboration, innovation, and growth in those they lead.

In a world driven by ambition and image, humility stands out as a symbol of authenticity. Research underscores its profound impact:

- A 2021 study found humble leaders are 30% more likely to build trust within teams, driving a 15% increase in employee engagement.
- A 2022 report revealed teams led by humble leaders produced 25% more innovative solutions than those under authoritarian leadership.
- Organizations with humble leaders also experience 17% lower employee turnover, according to Harvard Business Review.

Abraham Lincoln, a paragon of humble leadership, once said, *"I am not bound to win, but I am bound to be true."* His willingness to listen, admit mistakes, and serve the greater good exemplifies humility's power to inspire greatness.

Humble leadership empowers teams, nurtures loyalty, and leaves a lasting impact. As Brian Tracy reminds us, *"Successful people are always looking for opportunities to help others."* True leadership shines not by standing in the spotlight but by illuminating the path for others to succeed.

The Enduring Power of Humility in Leadership

As we wrap up this chapter, let me remind you that in today's dynamic world, humility is a cornerstone of effective leadership. Servant leadership—where leaders prioritize the needs of others and act with integrity—drives unparalleled success. Research from Harvard and Stanford confirms that humble leadership increases employee satisfaction by 25%, enhances productivity by 20%, and reduces turnover by 15% (Harvard Business Review, 2023).

Leaders like Howard Schultz, former CEO of Starbucks, exemplify this principle. By focusing on listening and serving his employees, Schultz transformed Starbucks into a global icon, fostering loyalty and long-term success. Such leaders prove that humility is not a weakness but a powerful strength that builds trust, fuels innovation, and empowers teams to excel.

As Ernest Hemingway said, *"There is nothing noble in being superior to your fellow man; true nobility is being superior to your former self."* True leadership isn't about personal gain—it's about lifting others and creating a legacy of collaboration and empowerment.

Takeaway: Embrace humility. Inspire trust. Foster greatness. The most impactful leaders build a future where everyone thrives together.

COURAGE OF THE SERVANT LEADER

Introduction

In this chapter, we delve into the essence of courage, exploring how it underpins the pursuit of leadership goals. Courage is not merely an attribute; it is the lifeblood of servant leadership. A leader's dreams and vision are only as robust as their courage. Without this fundamental trait, even the most promising goals may falter. Leaders who lack courage may possess ambitions but struggle to maintain a clear vision, passion, and belief. This chapter examines why courage is essential and how its absence can lead to mediocrity and failure.

"Courage is the ladder on which all the other virtues mount." — Clare Booth Luce

The Courage to Choose: Overcoming Fear to Lead Boldly

Fear and courage are eternal opposites. Fear sows doubt, while courage demands action. True leadership emerges when we confront fear, not avoid it. As Nelson Mandela said, *"Courage is not the absence of fear, but the triumph over it."*

I once faced a life-altering decision: accept a prestigious director role with comfort and status or pursue the uncertain path of entrepreneurship. Fear whispered warnings of failure, but courage, rooted in my vision, silenced those doubts. I chose the unknown, and though the road was challenging, it led to fulfillment and success far beyond titles or paychecks.

Courage is the key to unlocking creativity, resilience, and innovation. Fear may seek to paralyze us, but bold leaders rise above it, transforming challenges into opportunities. When courage leads, the impossible becomes attainable, and true potential is realized.

Takeaway: Leadership is choosing conviction over comfort. Conquer fear with courage, and you'll inspire others to do the same.

The Role of Vision in Courage

Courage thrives only where vision is clear and purpose is unwavering. Without a compelling vision, fear reigns, and courage falters. As Tony Robbins wisely puts it, *"Most people are not lazy. They simply have impotent goals—that is, goals that do not inspire them."* It's not about being the strongest or smartest; it's about having a goal that ignites your passion, fueling the courage to pursue it.

Your vision is the spark that lights the fire of courage. When your "why" is clear and compelling, courage follows, even in the face of adversity. The stronger your vision, the greater your courage. As the Bible teaches, *"Write the vision, and make it plain"* —for when your purpose is defined, fear has no power.

Takeaway: Vision fuels courage. Without a clear purpose, courage is just a distant dream. Lead with clarity, and fear will be left behind.

The Lion's Lesson: Courage from Vision

The lion, a symbol of unparalleled courage, teaches us a powerful lesson: its courage is driven by a clear vision. Though smaller than many of its prey, the lion's resolve is unwavering because it sees not just a meal, but an opportunity for survival. The greater the challenge, the stronger the lion's courage, showing us that true courage stems from a compelling vision.

As leaders, we must adopt the lion's perspective. Every challenge should be viewed as an opportunity for growth. Many falter due to uninspired goals, but as my father often said, *"Whatever a man wants to do, he will always find a chance or means."* A clear, compelling vision generates the courage to overcome any obstacle.

Takeaway: Courage is not about size or strength—it's about vision. Lead with purpose, and courage will follow.

Courage Fueled by Vision and Audacity

Visionary leaders like Dr. Martin Luther King Jr., Ellen Johnson Sirleaf, and Nelson Mandela show how courage, driven by a transformative vision, can change the world.

Dr. King's *"I Have a Dream"* speech continues to inspire the pursuit of racial equality. His courage in the face of violence demonstrated that true leadership embraces vulnerability and acts from love, not hate. His vision of a united, equal society empowered him to lead in the face of seemingly insurmountable obstacles.

Ellen Johnson Sirleaf, Africa's first female president, led post-war Liberia with relentless courage. Her words, *"If your dreams do not scare you, they are not big enough,"* reflect the audacity required to challenge the status quo. Her ambition to rebuild

Liberia after years of civil war shows that courage, fueled by a bold vision, drives societal progress.

Takeaway: The courage to lead begins with a vision that dares to be audacious. The larger the dream, the greater the courage required. Visionary leaders understand that fear is not a barrier, but a catalyst for growth and transformation.

Visionaries of Courage: Leaders Who Define Strength

Great leaders throughout history have proven that courage, when fueled by a clear and compelling vision, has the power to transform societies and change the world. These leaders not only endured immense hardships but also shaped history with their unwavering commitment to their purpose.

Nelson Mandela: The Courage of Endurance

Mandela's vision of a unified South Africa sustained him through 27 years of imprisonment. Upon his release, he dismantled apartheid and became the first Black president, proving that courage is not the absence of fear but the triumph over it. His leadership resonates with Proverbs 29:18: *"Where there is no vision, the people perish."*

Winston Churchill: Steadfast in the Face of War

During WWII, Churchill's unyielding vision of a free Europe galvanized Britain to stand firm against tyranny. His iconic words, *"We shall never surrender,"* are a testament to the power of vision in inspiring courage. As Joshua 1:9 affirms, *"Be strong and courageous... for the Lord your God will be with you wherever you go."*

Malala Yousafzai: Courage for Education

After surviving an assassination attempt, Malala's advocacy for girls' education in Pakistan became a beacon of courage. Her words, *"One child, one teacher, one book, one pen can change the world,"* reflect the transformative power of education. Proverbs 4:7 states, *"The beginning of wisdom is this: Get wisdom."*

Rosa Parks: Courageous Defiance

Rosa Parks' quiet act of defiance sparked a movement for civil rights, showing that courage doesn't always roar. Her refusal to give up her seat on a segregated bus became a powerful symbol of resistance. As MLK said, *"Courage is an inner resolution to go forward despite obstacles."*

Harriet Tubman: Vision for Freedom

Harriet Tubman risked her life repeatedly to lead enslaved people to freedom. Her vision of liberty was clear, and her courage knew no bounds. *"I freed a thousand slaves, and I could have freed a thousand more if only they knew they were slaves,"* she said, embodying the courage to fight for freedom. Philippians 4:13 reminds us, *"I can do all things through Christ who strengthens me."*

Barack Obama: Inspiring Change Through Hope

Barack Obama's presidency, built on a vision of hope and unity, inspired millions to believe in change. *"We are the ones we've been waiting for,"* he declared, urging others to act on their potential. Isaiah 40:31 echoes, *"But those who hope in the Lord will renew their strength."*

Nicholas Vujicic: Courage Over Adversity

Born without arms or legs, Nicholas Vujicic overcame incredible odds to become a motivational speaker and inspire millions. His vision of a life filled with purpose and possibility challenges us all. Maya Angelou wisely said, *"Courage is the most important of all the virtues because, without courage, you can't practice any other virtue consistently."*

Mahatma Gandhi: Courage for Freedom

Gandhi's unwavering commitment to nonviolence and his vision of a free India led to the end of British colonial rule. His leadership not only freed a nation but sparked movements for justice worldwide. As John F. Kennedy noted, *"Efforts and courage are not enough without purpose and direction."*

Takeaway:

True courage is rooted in vision. When leaders like Mandela, Churchill, and Malala pursued their visions, their courage transcended fear and shaped history. As these leaders show us, vision and courage are inseparable—together, they inspire change and empower others to rise above their challenges.

Courage Unleashed: Turning Vision into Victory

Courage is the driving force behind every great achievement. Fred Nightingale's seemingly impossible vision—to carve a path through a mountain that isolated his village—was ridiculed at first. Yet, his unwavering belief turned what others saw as folly into a reality, transforming his village into a thriving city. Fred's story teaches us that courage, when fueled by a clear vision, doesn't just change our circumstances—it inspires action in others, unlocking support and resources.

As Winston Churchill wisely said, *"Courage is what it takes to stand up and speak; courage is also what it takes to sit down and listen."* True leadership is not only about taking bold steps but also about empowering others with a shared vision.

As Jesus taught, *"If you have faith as small as a mustard seed, you can say to this mountain, 'Move from here to there,' and it will move. Nothing will be impossible for you"* (Matthew 17:20). With vision and courage, we can move mountains—both literal and metaphorical.

Takeaway: When courage is fueled by vision, it becomes a transformative force. Don't be afraid to take bold action, even when the path seems impossible. With a clear vision and the courage to act, you can move mountains and create lasting change, inspiring others to follow your lead.

The ERW 12-Point Model for Courage: Cultivating Leadership that Transforms

Courage is the heartbeat of great leadership. The ERW 12-Point Model serves as a blueprint for leaders who seek to inspire, motivate, and transform not only themselves but also those they lead. By embracing these principles, you can develop a leadership style rooted in courage that drives meaningful change and leaves a lasting impact.

1. **Vision**: A clear, purposeful vision sparks the courage to act. As I've learned, true leadership begins with daring to step into the unknown for a greater cause. "Where there is no vision, the people perish" (Proverbs 29:18). When aligned with our values, our vision ignites a fire within, fueling passion and inspiring others.
2. **Measurement**: Set clear, actionable goals. Every milestone, no matter how small, becomes a testament to courage and perseverance. Celebrating progress reinforces resilience and motivates everyone on the journey.
3. **Planning**: A structured roadmap guides us through uncertainty. Courage is staying true to our vision, even when obstacles arise. But adaptability is key—adjusting our sails without losing sight of our ultimate destination.
4. **The Long Game**: Transformation takes time. Courage is about embracing the journey, valuing persistence over immediate success. As challenges arise, they become

opportunities for growth, forging resilience in us and those we lead.

5. **Focus**: Courage demands prioritization. Focus on what matters most. Create an environment where dedication thrives. Your commitment inspires others to pursue their dreams with purpose.
6. **Mental Toughness**: Leadership is tested by adversity. Developing mental toughness means facing setbacks with clarity and resilience. Each obstacle is an opportunity to strengthen your resolve and lead with authenticity.
7. **Methodology**: Consistency is key. Small, deliberate actions compounded over time create monumental change. Embrace daily practices that reinforce your commitment and inspire others to join you on your mission.
8. **Spirituality**: A connection to your spiritual beliefs gives strength and guidance, especially in challenging times. Courage lies in confronting fears and embracing introspection. When we nurture our spiritual selves, we build a resilient foundation for leadership.
9. **Commitment**: Dedicate yourself fully to your vision. Courageous leadership demands sacrifice and focus. When you commit with passion, you inspire others to pursue their own missions, creating a collective momentum for change.
10. **Utterances**: Words have power. Proverbs 18:21 reminds us, *"The tongue has the power of life and death."* Speak words of encouragement and hope. Create an environment where courage and resilience thrive.
11. **Believe**: Faith in your vision is essential. "Faith is the substance of things hoped for, the evidence of things not seen" (Hebrews 11:1). Belief in yourself and your mission empowers others to believe, too.

12. **Gratitude**: Recognize and celebrate small victories. Gratitude fuels a courageous mindset. By acknowledging progress, we create a culture of empowerment where every step forward is cherished.

Takeaway: Courageous leadership is about commitment to a vision, resilience through challenges, and inspiring others through action and belief. Embrace these principles, and you will not only transform yourself but those around you. As John Quincy Adams said, *"If your actions inspire others to dream more, learn more, do more, and become more, you are a leader."* Lead with courage, and watch the impossible become inevitable.

The Legacy of Courage: Leaders Who Changed the World

Courage is not the absence of fear but the decision to act despite it. Throughout history, countless leaders have embodied this unwavering resolve, transforming the course of humanity with their boldness. From civil rights pioneers to philosophers who chose death over compromise, these leaders remind us that true courage is rooted in the commitment to one's beliefs, even in the face of immense adversity.

1. **Booker T. Washington** overcame the shackles of slavery to become an educator and advocate for vocational training, laying the foundation for future generations. His courage opened doors where none existed.
2. **Medgar Evers** gave his life for justice in the fight for voting rights. His sacrifice is a beacon, inspiring countless others to continue the struggle for equality and civil rights.
3. **Susan B. Anthony** never wavered in her pursuit of women's suffrage, challenging a society that sought to

silence her. Her tireless dedication to the cause of women's rights changed the fabric of America.

4. **Dietrich Bonhoeffer** stood against the Nazi regime, choosing death over silence in the face of evil. His courage to speak truth to power during one of the darkest times in history teaches us that faith and action are inseparable.
5. **Socrates** faced death rather than abandon his philosophical beliefs, marking him as a timeless symbol of intellectual courage. His refusal to compromise in the pursuit of truth continues to inspire thinkers and leaders across the world.
6. **Galileo** defied authority and faced house arrest for his belief in the heliocentric theory, forever changing the way we view the universe.
7. **Franklin D. Roosevelt** led the nation through the Great Depression and World War II while battling polio, proving that resilience and leadership are born from the most trying circumstances.
8. **Oprah Winfrey** broke barriers in media and philanthropy, using her platform to uplift marginalized voices and inspire social change.

These leaders and many others prove that courage is not limited to moments of grand achievement. It is in the small, daily choices to act with integrity, challenge the status quo, and persevere in the face of opposition. As **Winston Churchill** said, *"Courage is rightly esteemed the first of human qualities... because it is the quality which guarantees all others."*

As we reflect on their legacies, let us remember that the courage to pursue our dreams, challenge injustice, and act with integrity has the power to transform the world. The time to act is now.

Step forward with boldness, for the world awaits the impact of your courage.

THE MAGIC OF TEAMWORK: A BLUEPRINT FOR SUCCESS

INTRODUCTION: THE POWER OF TEAMWORK

In this chapter, we will explore the transformative power of teamwork and how to build a high-performance team that can elevate your organization to new heights. Whether you're scaling a company, growing a church, or enhancing the effectiveness of a government agency, understanding and harnessing the magic of teamwork is crucial. After all, nothing significant has ever been accomplished alone; great achievements are the result of collaborative effort.

Join me on this journey to uncover the principles of effective teamwork, and learn how you can cultivate a collaborative environment that empowers every member of your team to thrive. Together, let's explore how the collective strength of a united team can drive meaningful change and foster a spirit of innovation, resilience, and success.

As Helen Keller once said, *"Alone we can do so little; together we can do so much."* This timeless wisdom underscores the importance of synergy and shared purpose in achieving extraordinary results.

Teamwork is not just a buzzword; it is the driving force behind every successful endeavor. When individuals unite with a shared vision, they create a synergy that achieves the extraordinary.

"Teamwork makes the dream work." — John Maxwell

Building on this concept, it becomes clear that achieving greatness, outpacing competition, and fostering organizational growth all hinge on effective teamwork. When team members collaborate seamlessly, leveraging each other's strengths and skills, they become a powerhouse of innovation and productivity.

In such an environment, open communication, mutual support, and a shared vision transform individual efforts into collective triumphs. Challenges are no longer roadblocks—they become growth opportunities, fueled by shared determination and commitment.

"Two are better than one because they have a good reward for their labor. For if they fall, one will lift up his companion; but woe to him who is alone when he falls, for he has no one to help him up." — Ecclesiastes 4:9-10

As we delve deeper into the dynamics of teamwork, we will uncover the essential elements that forge cohesive teams—teams capable of overcoming any obstacle and propelling the organization toward unparalleled success.

Embracing the New Era of Teamwork

In the post-COVID-19 world, teams are more digital, dynamic, and diverse than ever. Amid challenges like political polarization and evolving work environments, the core principles of successful teamwork remain unchanged. True teamwork goes beyond assembling individuals; it demands a collective commitment to collaboration toward a shared goal.

This chapter will explore why some teams thrive while others struggle. High-performing teams are built on open communication, trust, and a sense of belonging. They leverage the diverse strengths of their members, creating an inclusive atmosphere where every voice is valued. In this rapidly changing landscape, adaptability and resilience are essential for teams navigating uncertainty.

By examining the practices that set successful teams apart, we'll uncover actionable strategies to foster cohesion, enabling teams to thrive in this new era. With a focus on collaboration and a shared vision, organizations can harness the full potential of their teams to drive meaningful impact.

"If one can put a thousand to flight, two can put ten thousand to flight." — Deuteronomy 32:30

This verse exemplifies the power of teamwork, where unity amplifies strength and the collective effort can achieve far more than individual action.

TYPES OF TEAMS: UNDERSTANDING THE SPECTRUM

In the realm of teamwork, recognizing the different types of teams and their impact on organizational success is essential. After reflecting on various team dynamics, I've identified three primary types that shape outcomes:

High-Performance Teams

These teams consistently achieve outstanding results and drive organizational growth. They excel through exceptional collaboration, motivation, and leadership, fostering an environment where innovation flourishes. I deeply admire how high-performance teams leverage each member's strengths to achieve a shared vision.

Low-Performance Teams

Operating at a slower pace, these teams may struggle to create significant impact. Their limited effectiveness can hinder progress and undermine the organization's overall success. I've seen that when motivation wanes and collaboration weaken, the potential for greatness often remains untapped.

Dysfunctional Teams

These teams, the most detrimental to an organization, lack cohesion and productivity, posing a serious threat to success. I believe that when communication falters and trust is absent, the consequences can be severe—not only for the team but for the entire organization.

Understanding these distinctions is crucial for any leader seeking to cultivate a culture of collaboration and excellence. This insight allows leaders to identify areas for improvement and implement strategies that foster high performance, transforming challenges into opportunities for growth and success.

UNLEASHING THE POWER OF TEAMWORK: BUILDING HIGH-PERFORMANCE TEAMS FOR UNSTOPPABLE SUCCESS

Teamwork is the key to achieving greatness in any organization. This chapter, *"The Magic of Teamwork,"* will guide you in building high-performance teams that drive success. Whether in business, a church, or a government agency, no major achievement happens alone.

High-performing teams thrive on clear goals, open communication, trust, and shared purpose. Leaders inspire collaboration, empowering teams to exceed expectations and drive innovation. This chapter will explore how to create resilient teams that deliver lasting success.

"Alone we can do so little; together we can do so much." – Helen Kelle

The Impact of High-Performance Teams

Companies like Google, Apple, Amazon, Facebook, Walmart, and Tesla have revolutionized the world thanks to their high-performance teams. These tech giants exemplify how collaboration and effective team dynamics can lead to market dominance and superior performance. By fostering an environment that encourages creativity and open communication, they empower their teams to push boundaries and drive innovation. **In turn**, this environment encourages groundbreaking achievements that set these companies apart.

Moreover, studies show that groups can innovate more effectively, deliver faster results, achieve higher productivity, and solve problems more efficiently than individuals working alone. High-performance teams harness diverse perspectives, combining unique skill sets and experiences to tackle challenges from multiple angles. **As a result**, this synergy not only enhances problem-solving capabilities but also cultivates a culture of continuous improvement, where team members feel valued and motivated to contribute their best.

Furthermore, the impact of such teamwork extends beyond immediate results. It creates a ripple effect that influences company culture, employee engagement, and long-term success.

"If you take out the team in teamwork, it's just work that's left. Now, who wants that?"

— Matthew Woodring Stover

CHARACTERISTICS OF HIGH-PERFORMANCE TEAMS

Exceptional Performance

High-performance teams consistently achieve outstanding results, excelling in their fields and driving significant growth. Setting ambitious goals and maintaining a relentless pursuit of excellence are non-negotiables for lasting impact. As Vince Lombardi said, *"Perfection is not attainable, but if we chase perfection, we can catch excellence."*

Collaborative Leadership

Leaders in these teams delegate effectively and inspire rather than micromanage. They act as motivators and facilitators, empowering members to reach their potential. Recognizing contributions, much like celebrating an athlete's victories, reinforces motivation. John Maxwell aptly noted, *"A leader is one who knows the way, goes the way, and shows the way."*

Equitable Voice

Every member of a high-performance team has an equal opportunity to contribute. When all voices are heard, creativity and engagement flourish. Harvard research confirms that inclusivity drives productivity and innovation. As Margaret Mead observed, *"Never doubt that a small group of thoughtful, committed citizens can change the world."*

Constructive Conflict Management

High-performance teams view conflict as an opportunity, addressing it with humility and a team-first mindset. Constructive conflict strengthens relationships and leads to better outcomes. As Patrick Lencioni said, *"Conflict is not the enemy of teamwork; it is its necessary component."*

Transparent Communication

Open and honest communication is the backbone of trust and collaboration. Transparency ensures clarity, prevents misunderstandings, and fosters alignment. Peter Drucker reminds us, *"The most important thing in communication is hearing what isn't said."*

Emotional Intelligence

Team members exhibit emotional intelligence, demonstrating empathy, self-awareness, and interpersonal sensitivity. These traits create a harmonious and supportive environment. Daniel Goleman, a pioneer in emotional intelligence, stated, *"Emotional intelligence is the sine qua non of leadership."*

Humility

Mutual respect and humility define high-performing teams. Members prioritize collective strength over individual egos, lifting each other to success. As C.S. Lewis remarked, *"Humility is not thinking less of yourself, but thinking of yourself less."*

Loyalty

Loyalty binds teams together, fostering inclusion, dedication, and psychological safety. Members work selflessly for the collective good. Simon Sinek captures this spirit: *"A team is not a group of people who work together. A team is a group of people who trust each other."*

Effective Time Management

High-performance teams balance productivity with meaningful interactions. They manage time wisely while maintaining positive relationships. As Benjamin Franklin wisely advised, *"Lost time is never found again."*

Accountability and Transparency

Accountability fosters trust and precision, ensuring every member takes ownership of their responsibilities. Transparency reinforces this trust, creating a culture of integrity. As Stephen Covey said, *"Accountability breeds response-ability."*

High-performance teams are not born but built through intentionality, trust, and shared commitment. These characteristics serve as the foundation for achieving extraordinary success.

Embracing High-Performance Teams

Building on this foundation, high-performance teams demonstrate what is possible when collaboration, commitment, and shared vision align. These teams embody traits like emotional intelligence, humility, and accountability—essential elements that drive success.

Creating an environment where these characteristics thrive requires intentional leadership. By fostering trust, encouraging innovation, and celebrating achievements, leaders unlock their teams' potential, empowering members to embrace challenges and pursue shared goals with passion.

A modern example of this is Tim Cook, CEO of Apple. Cook has emphasized the importance of collaboration and inclusivity since taking the helm. Under his leadership, Apple has fostered a culture where teamwork and diverse perspectives drive innovation and operational excellence. His approach ensures that every team member contributes to Apple's continued success.

In a world demanding agility and resilience, high-performance teams are indispensable. They navigate complexity with grace and inspire excellence, proving that collaboration and courage can achieve the seemingly unattainable. The journey to high performance is not merely a goal but a transformative commitment to excellence that reshapes teams and organizations alike.

Low-performance Teams

Low-performance teams present unique challenges that can significantly hinder an organization's success. These teams, marked by disengagement, poor communication, and lack of accountability, often struggle to meet their objectives, ultimately affecting overall productivity and morale. I firmly believe that recognizing these characteristics is the first step toward improvement.

By addressing the root causes of low performance—such as unclear goals, inadequate support, and ineffective leadership—we can foster an environment where team members feel valued and empowered. Encouraging open communication, promoting a shared vision, and establishing accountability can transform low-performance teams into vibrant, high-performing units.

15 Characteristics of Low-Performance Teams

1. Lack of Direction: Low-performance teams often lack a clear vision or goals. This ambiguity leads to confusion and inefficiency, as team members may not understand their roles or the team's purpose. I believe that without a defined direction, it's challenging for any team to succeed.
2. Lack of Vision: Members of low-performance teams often lack a clear understanding of the organization's overall vision, leading to misalignment and disengagement from broader goals.
3. Poor Communication: Ineffective communication is a hallmark of low-performance teams. Misunderstandings, incomplete information, and lack

of open dialogue can create a toxic environment where collaboration falters. I've seen how poor communication can derail progress and erode trust.

4. Limited Collaboration: Team members may work in silos rather than collaborating effectively. This isolation stifles innovation and prevents the sharing of diverse perspectives, ultimately diminishing the team's overall performance. I've found that collaboration is essential for harnessing collective intelligence.
5. Lack of Accountability: In low-performance teams, members often avoid taking responsibility for their actions. This absence of accountability can lead to missed deadlines, unfulfilled commitments, and a culture of blame. I firmly believe that accountability is vital for fostering a sense of ownership within a team.
6. Resistance to Change: Low-performance teams are typically resistant to change and innovation. This reluctance can stem from fear of failure or a lack of confidence, resulting in stagnation. I recognize that embracing change is crucial for growth and adaptability in today's fast-paced environment.
7. Unclear Roles and Responsibilities: When team members are unsure of their roles, it can lead to overlaps, gaps, and frustration. Low-performance teams often suffer from a lack of clarity about who is responsible for what, impeding progress and efficiency. I emphasize the importance of defining roles to enhance accountability and collaboration.
8. Negative Attitudes: Pessimism and negativity can permeate low-performance teams, creating a toxic culture that stifles motivation and engagement. I've observed that a negative mindset not only impacts individual performance but also undermines the entire team's morale.

9. Ineffective Conflict Resolution: Low-performance teams often avoid conflict or handle it poorly, leading to unresolved issues that fester over time. This avoidance can create tension and hinder productive collaboration. I believe that addressing conflicts constructively is essential for maintaining a healthy team dynamic.
10. Low Motivation and Engagement: Members of low-performance teams often lack motivation and commitment. This disengagement can stem from a lack of recognition, unfulfilling work, or feeling undervalued. I've seen how fostering a culture of recognition and appreciation can reinvigorate a team's spirit.
11. Inconsistent Performance: Low-performance teams may deliver erratic results, fluctuating between bursts of productivity and periods of stagnation. This inconsistency reflects a lack of cohesive effort and shared commitment to goals. I hold that establishing consistent standards and expectations is key to achieving sustained success.
12. Personal Competition: In low-performance teams, individual success often overshadows collective goals.
13. Members compete to outshine each other, losing sight of the team's overall objectives and undermining collaboration.
14. Power Struggles: Power struggles are common in low-performance teams, where personal achievement takes precedence over team success. This creates a fractured environment where collaboration is hindered.
15. Disconnection: Members struggle to see how their contributions fit into the larger strategy, feeling disconnected from high-level decisions and the team's mission.

16. Autocratic Leadership: Leaders of low-performance teams often make decisions unilaterally, stifling team input and innovation. This autocratic approach limits the potential for collaborative success.

Leaders need to invest in team development and cultivate a culture of collaboration and mutual respect. When we commit to nurturing our teams, we not only enhance their performance but also create a foundation for sustainable success. Embracing this journey will lead to not only individual growth but also collective achieve-mints that propel our organizations forward. Together, we can turn the tide on low performance and unlock the full potential of our teams.

Dysfunctional Teams

Dysfunctional teams represent a significant challenge within organizations. They not only impede progress but can also create a toxic culture that affects morale and productivity. By understanding the characteristics of these teams, we can recognize the importance of fostering a supportive and collaborative environment. As we reflect on these dynamics, it becomes clear that we must cultivate trust, communication, and accountability to shift from dysfunction to high performance. The journey may be challenging, but the rewards of transforming a dysfunctional team into a thriving, high-performance unit are well worth the effort

12 CHARACTERISTICS OF DYSFUNCTIONAL TEAMS

1. Lack of Trust: Dysfunctional teams often operate in an environment where members do not trust one another. This lack of trust inhibits open communication and collaboration.

2. Poor Communication: Communication breakdowns are common in dysfunctional teams, leading to misunderstandings and missed opportunities. Team members may withhold information or fail to engage in meaningful dialogue.
3. Avoidance of Conflict: Members may avoid addressing conflicts or disagreements, resulting in unresolved issues that fester and disrupt team dynamics. This avoidance can lead to passive-aggressive behavior and resentment.
4. Absence of Commitment: When team members don't feel heard or valued, they may lack commitment to team goals. This disengagement can diminish motivation and hinder progress.
5. Accountability Issues: Dysfunctional teams often struggle with accountability. Members may shift blame or refuse to take responsibility for their actions, undermining team cohesion and effectiveness. Avoidance of accountability is prevalent in dysfunctional teams. Members evade responsibility, leading to finger-pointing and procrastination, which hampers progress and productivity.
6. Inconsistent Goals: Lack of clarity around team objectives can lead to confusion and misalignment. Dysfunctional teams often have members pulling in different directions, which can stall progress.
7. Low Morale: A toxic environment can drain the energy and enthusiasm of team members, leading to decreased productivity and engagement. This often results in high turnover rates, challenges in attracting new talent, and a decline in overall organizational performance.
8. Resistance to Change: Dysfunctional teams may resist new ideas or changes in direction, clinging to outdated practices and hindering innovation.

9. Micromanagement: Leaders may feel compelled to micromanage due to a lack of trust, which stifles creativity and demotivates team members. This approach can create a culture of dependency rather than empowerment.
10. **Failure to Learn from Mistakes:** Dysfunctional teams often fail to reflect on their experiences, missing opportunities for growth and improvement. This lack of learning can perpetuate cycles of poor performance.
11. **Focus on Personal Gain:** Dysfunctional teams are often more concerned with individual recognition than with achieving collective goals. This self-centered approach undermines team success and fosters burnout.
12. **Lack of Commitment:** A lack of commitment to the team's objectives and overall success leads to disengagement and suboptimal performance. Team members may not contribute fully or engage in critical discussions.

Dysfunctional teams must transform into high-performance teams to enhance productivity, foster collaboration, and achieve organizational goals effectively. High-performance teams operate with clear communication, trust, and shared accountability, minimizing conflicts and inefficiencies. This transformation is essential to unlock the team's potential, improve morale, retain talent, and drive sustained success in a competitive environment.

CULTIVATING HIGH-PERFORMANCE TEAMS THROUGH SERVANT LEADERSHIP

"If you take out the team in teamwork, it's just work that's left. Now, who wants that?" — Matthew Woodring Stover

The modern servant leader prioritizes the needs of their team, creating an environment where collaboration, trust, and accountability thrive. By embracing principles such as equitable voice, transparent communication, and emotional intelligence, servant leaders empower their teams to achieve extraordinary outcomes.

Understanding the dynamics of high-performance teams equips leaders with the tools to not only identify but actively foster such environments. Striving for greatness in our organizations starts with recognizing that the foundation of effective teamwork is servant leadership. By supporting our teams, celebrating their victories, and guiding them through challenges, we can cultivate a culture of excellence that drives us toward our shared vision.

WAYS TO CULTIVATE HIGH-PERFORMANCE TEAMS THROUGH SERVANT LEADERSHIP

1. **Model Humility**
   - **Actionable Steps:**
     - Admit mistakes openly to demonstrate vulnerability and authenticity.
     - Seek feedback from the team on your leadership style and decisions.
     - Acknowledge the contributions of team members before highlighting your own achievements.
2. **Encourage Collaboration**
   - **Actionable Steps:**
     - Implement collaborative tools and practices (e.g., brainstorming sessions, project management software).
     - Design team-building activities that foster trust and connection.

    - Assign cross-functional projects to encourage diverse skill sets to work together.

3. **Prioritize Development**
    - **Actionable Steps:**
        - Create individual development plans aligned with team members' career aspirations.
        - Offer access to training programs, certifications, and workshops.
        - Pair team members with mentors to foster growth and shared knowledge.
4. **Foster Psychological Safety**
    - **Actionable Steps:**
        - Actively listen to team members and validate their ideas, even if they are not immediately actionable.
        - Set norms for constructive feedback and conflict resolution.
        - Celebrate learning moments from failures to encourage risk-taking without fear.
5. **Set Clear Goals**
    - **Actionable Steps:**
        - Use SMART criteria (Specific, Measurable, Achievable, Relevant, Time-bound) to define goals.
        - Regularly revisit goals to ensure alignment with evolving team and organizational priorities.
        - Break down long-term objectives into manageable milestones.
6. **Celebrate Achievements**
    - **Actionable Steps:**
        - Establish a recognition program for both individual and team accomplishments.
        - Host informal celebrations or team lunches to mark project completions or milestones.

        - Share success stories with the broader organization to spotlight team efforts.

7. **Facilitate Open Communication**
    - **Actionable Steps:**
        - Hold regular check-ins and team meetings where everyone is encouraged to share updates.
        - Use anonymous surveys to gather honest feedback on team dynamics and leadership.
        - Clearly articulate expectations and provide timely updates on organizational changes.
8. **Embrace Diversity**
    - **Actionable Steps:**
        - Actively recruit team members with diverse backgrounds and experiences.
        - Provide unconscious bias training to ensure inclusive decision-making.
        - Celebrate cultural milestones and events to foster a sense of belonging.
9. **Lead by Example**
    - **Actionable Steps:**
        - Demonstrate punctuality, preparation, and accountability in your own work.
        - Show empathy by taking time to understand team members' challenges and concerns.
        - Uphold integrity by being consistent in words and actions.
10. **Encourage Autonomy**
    - **Actionable Steps:**
        - Define clear roles and responsibilities but allow team members the flexibility to choose their approach.
        - Delegate meaningful tasks that align with individual strengths.

        - Check in periodically to provide guidance without micromanaging.
11. **Maintain Focus on the Team's Well-Being**
    - **Actionable Steps:**
        - Encourage regular breaks and support flexible working hours when possible.
        - Provide resources for mental health and wellness, such as access to counseling or mindfulness programs.
        - Regularly check in on team members' workloads to avoid burnout.
12. **Adapt and Innovate**
    - **Actionable Steps:**
        - Stay informed about industry trends and share relevant insights with the team.
        - Encourage the team to experiment with new tools, methods, or strategies.
        - Foster a mindset of agility by celebrating quick pivots and creative problem-solving.
13. **Cultivate a Culture of Feedback**
    - Create a feedback loop where both leaders and team members give and receive constructive input.
    - Use 360-degree feedback tools to gather holistic perspectives.
14. **Promote Cross-Training**
    - Rotate roles within the team periodically to build versatility and resilience.
    - Encourage knowledge sharing sessions to distribute expertise across the team.
15. **Develop a Strong Onboarding Process**
    - Provide clear expectations, resources, and introductions to new team members to set them up for success.

- Assign a buddy or mentor to help new hires integrate into the team culture.

16. **Align Values with Actions**
    - Frequently revisit the team's mission and values to ensure alignment with daily operations.
    - Lead discussions on how team goals contribute to the larger organizational vision.
17. **Measure and Celebrate Progress**
    - Use key performance indicators (KPIs) to track team success and make data-driven decisions.
    - Share visual progress reports during meetings to keep everyone informed and motivated.
18. **Encourage Creativity and Innovation**
    - Set aside dedicated time for brainstorming sessions or hackathons.
    - Recognize and reward innovative ideas, even if they're not immediately implemented.
19. **Resolve Conflicts Constructively**
    - Use mediation techniques to address conflicts and ensure all parties feel heard.
    - Document resolutions and learnings from conflicts to improve future team dynamics.

By implementing these strategies, servant leaders not only enhance team performance but also create a sustainable, thriving culture that empowers individuals to excel. Would you like further details on any specific strategy?

Unlocking Extraordinary Potential: The Blueprint for High-Performance Teams

High-performance teams are the foundation of extraordinary achievements, propelling organizations to new heights and driving sustainable growth. These teams consistently exceed expectations by aligning around shared goals that surpass individual ambitions. By harnessing each member's unique strengths, fostering transparent communication, and cultivating a culture of trust and accountability, they create a dynamic synergy that fuels innovation and success. In essence, high-performance teams unlock their members' full potential, enabling organizations to adapt, thrive, and excel in an ever-evolving landscape.

TRANSFORMATIVE LEADERSHIP

The leader of a high-performance team is a true catalyst for success, embodying a collaborative approach that elevates the entire group. Rather than relying on authority, these leaders empower their team, inspiring greatness through action and example. They are not micromanagers, but motivators and coaches, fostering a culture of trust and mutual respect. Just as star athletes like LeBron James are celebrated for their extraordinary contributions, every exceptional team member deserves recognition and reward. This creates a powerful environment where everyone is driven to achieve their highest potential.

- **The Power of Voice**

Harvard Business School research highlights that for a team to thrive, every member must have an equal voice. When individuals feel heard and valued, their engagement and productivity increase significantly.

A servant leader is key to this process, ensuring that each team member's voice is respected. By fostering a culture of inclusivity, diverse perspectives are embraced, leading to innovative solutions. This creates a collaborative environment where creativity and synergy flourish.

"For the body does not consist of one member but of many." – 1 Corinthians 12:14

Constructive Conflict Resolution in High-Performance Teams

High-performance teams view conflict as a powerful catalyst for growth, not as a hindrance. A prime example is Pixar Animation Studios, renowned for its culture of constructive conflict. Early in its development, Pixar's leadership, including Ed Catmull and John Lasseter, fostered an environment where every team member, from animators to engineers, was encouraged to voice differing opinions. This openness led to intense debates during the creation of films like *Toy Story*, where the team's diverse perspectives were seen as essential to refining ideas and making breakthroughs.

Rather than letting disagreements tear the team apart, Pixar's leadership saw them as opportunities to strengthen the final product. High-performance teams, like Pixar's, navigate conflict with humility, focusing on the collective good rather than personal gain. These teams embrace conflict constructively, which not only resolves issues but enhances team cohesion and drives innovation.

Coaching on Conflict Resolution: To effectively resolve conflict in high-performance teams, it's essential to:

1. **Encourage Open Dialogue**: Leaders should create a safe environment where team members feel comfortable sharing differing views. Encourage active listening and respect, ensuring all voices are heard.
2. **Focus on Common Goals**: Remind the team of the bigger picture—the shared vision and objectives. Keeping everyone focused on these collective goals

shifts the focus from individual differences to collaborative problem-solving.

3. **Embrace Diverse Perspectives**: Instead of avoiding differing opinions, value them. Diverse perspectives often lead to creative breakthroughs and improved solutions.
4. **Stay Solution-Focused**: During conflicts, shift the conversation from blame to finding solutions. Focus on what can be done to move forward rather than dwelling on the problem.
5. **Model Constructive Behavior**: As a leader or team member, demonstrate calm and respectful conflict resolution. Your behavior sets the tone for others to follow.

In high-performance teams, conflict is viewed not as something to be feared, but as a tool for innovation and growth. When handled constructively, it can transform challenges into opportunities, leading to stronger collaboration and breakthrough achievements.

Transparent Communication in High-Performance Teams

Effective communication is the bedrock of high-performance teams. Open, honest, and frequent exchanges build trust and prevent the erosion of morale that secrecy can breed. In high-performing environments, transparency is not just a tool; it's a core value that drives success. When team members are kept in the loop, they feel empowered and engaged, fostering a deeper sense of ownership and accountability.

Leaders play a crucial role in championing transparency. They must ensure that all key information is easily accessible and that everyone on the team feels secure in sharing their thoughts, ideas, and concerns. This openness creates an environment where collaboration flourishes, as individuals are more likely to contribute when they know their voices are valued.

For instance, in companies like *Google*, where transparency is ingrained in the culture, employees are encouraged to freely share ideas and provide feedback, regardless of rank or position. This constant flow of information sparks innovation, improves decision-making, and strengthens relationships among team members.

Transparent communication goes beyond the exchange of information—it builds trust, nurtures creativity, and fuels collaboration. When leaders prioritize open dialogue, teams not only work more efficiently but also thrive in an atmosphere that encourages innovation and collaboration.

Emotional Intelligence in High-Performance Teams

High-performance teams thrive on emotional intelligence. Team members are self-aware, empathetic, and skilled at managing both their own emotions and those of others. This emotional sensitivity creates a supportive environment where individuals can excel both professionally and personally. By fostering strong interpersonal bonds, emotional intelligence strengthens team cohesion and resilience, enhancing the team's collective effectiveness and drive.

Humility and Respect in High-Performance Teams

Humility is a core trait of high-performance teams. Both members and leaders show deep respect for one another, prioritizing mutual support over competition. The most effective team members uplift others, fostering a culture of respect that drives collaboration and progress. This humility strengthens relationships, creating an environment where the team thrives together.

Loyalty in High-Performance Teams

Loyalty is the cornerstone of high-performance teams. Team members are committed not just to achieving success but also to supporting each other's well-being. As Harry Truman said, "It is amazing what you can accomplish if you do not care who gets the credit." This selfless dedication creates a strong bond within the team, enhancing performance and fostering a deep sense of belonging.

Mastery of Time Management in High-Performance Teams

Effective time management is crucial for high-performance teams. They prioritize tasks, maintain focus, and ensure that every moment spent aligns with the team's goals. This discipline boosts productivity, drives progress, and reinforces the team's commitment to excellence.

Embracing Accountability in a High-Performance Team

Accountability is fundamental to high-performance teams. Members take ownership of their actions and contributions, cultivating trust and transparency. This clarity in processes and results boosts confidence and drives success, creating a culture where everyone is committed to achieving the team's shared vision.

Case Study: The Whitney Jones Furniture Company

The Whitney Jones Furniture Company, established as a staple in the industry for decades, found itself in a troubling decline despite its reputation for high-quality products. Sales were plummeting, and the company's once-vibrant presence in the market had waned. Internal assessments revealed that the company's culture had become stagnant and territorial. Employees were working in silos, resistant to change, and communication had broken down. Leadership had failed to embrace the rapidly changing business environment, which included shifts in consumer preferences and the rise of digital marketing.

When Paul Wilson was appointed CEO, he was immediately struck by the company's internal challenges. The culture, which had once thrived under traditional practices, was now hindering the company's growth and adaptability. Wilson recognized that the company's core issues went beyond just product quality; there was a lack of collaboration, an aversion to risk-taking, and an absence of innovation.

Revitalizing the Company Culture

Wilson's first major initiative was to address the stagnant culture. He introduced a team-based approach to operations, encouraging collaboration between departments that had previously operated in isolation. This approach helped break down the silos and fostered an environment where ideas were shared freely, allowing for cross-pollination of ideas. He implemented regular team meetings and brainstorming sessions to ensure that employees at all levels were contributing to the company's direction and success.

Wilson also focused on diversifying the team to build a more dynamic workforce. By bringing in individuals with varied backgrounds and skill sets, he introduced fresh perspectives that challenged the status quo. This new diversity of thought sparked innovation, as team members were more willing to take calculated risks and think outside the box.

Digital Transformation and Innovation

Recognizing the critical need for modernization, Wilson pushed for a digital transformation of the company. The first step was implementing digital marketing strategies to reach a broader audience. The company had previously relied on traditional methods such as print advertising and word of mouth. By embracing social media platforms, search engine optimization, and online advertising, Whitney Jones Furniture expanded its reach to a younger demographic and engaged with customers in ways it had never done before.

Alongside marketing innovations, Wilson led efforts to revamp the product line, which had grown outdated and lacked appeal to the modern consumer. He invested in innovative product design, introducing contemporary styles and more sustainable materials that resonated with environmentally-conscious buyers. Collaborating with design experts, the company began offering customizable furniture, allowing customers to choose fabrics, colors, and finishes to suit their individual tastes.

The Result: A Reborn Company

The results of Wilson's leadership were nothing short of remarkable. The team-based, collaborative culture he introduced began to pay off, with employees motivated to contribute their best ideas and work towards a shared vision. The digital marketing efforts proved successful, driving an increase in online sales and improving the company's visibility in a competitive market. As a result of these efforts, the company saw a dramatic recovery from its financial losses. Within two years, Whitney Jones Furniture had not only regained its previous profitability but had achieved unprecedented growth, surpassing sales figures from its peak years.

The company's success was no longer attributed solely to the quality of its products, but also to its ability to adapt to new market demands and foster a culture of collaboration and innovation. The revamped team dynamic and the strategic digital transformation created a strong foundation for future growth, positioning the company as a leader in the furniture industry once again.

CONCLUSION

The case of Whitney Jones Furniture illustrates the transformative power of embracing a team-based, collaborative culture, coupled with a willingness to innovate and adapt to new trends. Under Paul Wilson's leadership, the company successfully navigated its challenges and emerged as a more resilient and profitable organization. This case serves as a valuable example of how strong leadership, combined with an openness to change and collaboration, can reinvigorate even the most established companies and propel them into a successful future.

The ERW Model for Building High-Performance Teams

Leadership

At the core of every high-performance team is a servant leader —someone who embodies humility, transparency, and connection. Through a SWOT analysis, they leverage strengths and address weaknesses, guiding the team toward a shared purpose. True leadership isn't about authority; it's about uplifting others.

Accountability and Feedback

Accountability builds trust. Feedback is essential for growth, transforming mistakes into lessons. A culture of accountability ignites ownership and drives a collective desire to excel, ensuring continuous improvement.

Trust

Mutual trust fuels collaboration and growth. By fostering vulnerability and authenticity, teams unite in their pursuit of excellence, creating an environment where ideas flow freely, and creativity thrives.

Transparency and Clearly Defined Goals

Clear communication fosters alignment. High-performance teams thrive when everyone understands not just *what* they're doing but *why*. This transparency breeds commitment, transforming individual tasks into shared achievements.

Attitude

A positive attitude is contagious. By cultivating optimism and encouragement, leaders can inspire resilience and unity, turning challenges into opportunities and uniting teams toward a common vision.

Boundaries

Defined roles and responsibilities create clarity and security. When team members understand their limitations, they can confidently collaborate, empowering individuals and strengthening the collective.

Motivation and Empowerment

Empowering team members to take on new responsibilities fuels passion and creativity. Motivated individuals contribute to a culture of excellence, transforming challenges into opportunities.

Alignment and Standard Operating Procedures

Aligning strengths with organizational goals ensures effective execution. Standard operating procedures provide a roadmap for success, reinforcing a shared commitment to achieving objectives.

Conflict

Healthy conflict sparks innovation. Managing conflict with

grace allows diverse opinions to enrich decision-making, pushing teams to new heights and delivering the best solutions.

Supportive Organizational Culture

A culture that values diversity, creativity, and risk-taking nurtures growth. By creating an environment where team members feel safe to express ideas, we unlock the full potential of each individual.

The **ERW Model** serves as a blueprint for servant leaders committed to fostering collaboration and excellence. By embracing these principles, we enhance team performance and inspire a legacy of courage, resilience, and achievement.

The Essence of High-Performance Teams

Collective Effort

High-performance teams are built on a shared vision, where individual efforts fuel collective success. As Andrew Carnegie said, "Teamwork is the ability to collaborate toward a shared vision... It is the fuel that allows ordinary people to attain uncommon results." This spirit transforms ordinary contributions into extraordinary outcomes.

Transformative Leadership

True leaders in high-performance teams inspire, empower, and serve. They create an environment where every voice matters, fostering innovation through diversity and inclusion. Leadership is about guiding, not commanding, and this approach drives teams toward progress.

The Value of Vision and Commitment

A clear vision and commitment to a shared goal are the foundation of success, as seen with companies like Amazon and Google. Vince Lombardi said, "Individual commitment to a group effort—that is what makes teamwork, a company work." When every member is aligned with the vision, possibilities are limitless.

The Role of Each Member

In a high-performance team, every member plays a vital role. As with legends like Michael Jordan and LeBron James, team success is built on collective strength, not individual prowess. Recognizing each member's value fosters seamless collaboration.

Building Each Other Up

Mutual support is the hallmark of high-performance teams. As Forbes highlights, "High-performance team members work to build each other up." This shared care and motivation elevate the team, turning challenges into shared successes.

Embracing Accountability and Transparency

Transparency and accountability build trust and align the team with its goals. Open communication ensures every member understands their role and the collective mission, enabling seamless collaboration.

Conflict as a Catalyst for Growth

Conflict, when approached constructively, sparks creativity and strengthens teams. Embracing differing opinions leads to innovation and fosters team cohesion, turning potential discord into a powerful force for progress.

The Power of Emotional Intelligence

Emotional intelligence enables team members to manage emotions, fostering a supportive environment where both personal and professional growth can thrive. This deeper connection enhances collaboration and understanding.

Loyalty and Respect

Loyalty and respect are the foundation of a cohesive team. As Phil Jackson said, "The strength of the team is each member. The strength of each member is the team." Mutual respect strengthens bonds, enabling teams to overcome challenges together.

High-performance teams thrive by harnessing collective effort, transformative leadership, and a culture of loyalty and respect. By embracing these principles, teams can achieve remarkable success and leave a lasting legacy of excellence.

"The strength of the team is each member. The strength of each member is the team."

— Phil Jackson

In fostering high-performance teams, remember: that the magic of teamwork elevates each individual while achieving collective greatness. By embracing these values, you unlock the innovation potential, surpassing goals, and propelling your team to new heights.

The Boston Celtics' 2024 Journey to Championship Glory Through Teamwork

The Boston Celtics' 2023/2024 NBA Championship run is a powerful testament to the transformative power of teamwork. From the outset, the team embraced a singular vision—not just to win games but to forge an unbreakable bond. Under head coach Joe Mazzulla's leadership, the Celtics became more than just a group of individual talents—they became a family, united by their shared dreams and unwavering commitment.

Rising to the Challenge

When the Celtics faced the Miami Heat in the Eastern Conference Finals, they were tested like never before. Trailing in the series, the team could have easily fractured under pressure. Instead, they rallied together. In the decisive Game 6, they executed a miraculous fourth-quarter comeback, demonstrating what they had built: a team that played for each other. As Jayson Tatum declared, "We play for each other. Together, we are unstoppable," this mantra ignited a fire within the team that carried them forward.

The Championship Moment

Moving into the NBA Finals against the Denver Nuggets, the stakes were higher than ever. Game 4 became a battleground where every possession mattered. In those tense final moments, players like Marcus Smart and Robert Williams stepped up, making clutch plays that turned the tide in the Celtics' favor. As the final buzzer sounded, the Celtics' victory wasn't just a win; it was the culmination of their collective journey. Tatum, overwhelmed with emotion, proclaimed, "This is for everyone who believed in us."

A Legacy of Togetherness

However, the Celtics' triumph was more than just a title; it was a legacy of teamwork and sacrifice. They demonstrated that true greatness is rooted in the connections we forge and the willingness to uplift each other. Through their journey, the team transformed challenges into opportunities and proved that when individuals come together with purpose and heart, they can achieve the extraordinary.

In conclusion, the 2024 Boston Celtics will be remembered not only as champions but as a beacon of what teamwork can accomplish. Their journey serves as a reminder of the core principles of high-performance teams: collaboration, trust, and servant leadership. In a world full of challenges, their story reminds us that greatness is achieved through collective effort. By lifting one another up, we can accomplish the extraordinary.

Prioritizing the Growth of Team Members

When leaders prioritize the growth and empowerment of their team members, they create a culture that moves beyond traditional hierarchies. By shifting from a command-and-control mindset to a servant-first approach, they transform how teams interact, communicate, and perform. In this environment, every voice is valued, and each contribution is recognized. Together, team members forge a path toward a shared vision that is greater than the sum of its parts.

The Power of Unity in High-Performance Teams

Reflecting on the remarkable achievements of high-performance teams—from sports fields to corporate boardrooms—it becomes clear that their success is rooted in the core principles of empathy, humility, and mutual respect. These teams exemplify the transformative power of unity. When individuals come together with a common purpose, extraordinary outcomes are not only possible but inevitable.

A Catalyst for Transformation

In essence, the power of teamwork, fueled by servant leadership, becomes a catalyst for transformation, resilience, and sustained success. High-performance teams don't just achieve goals; they drive exponential growth for organizations. By cultivating a culture of collaboration and shared success, these teams accelerate innovation, enhance productivity, and unlock new business opportunities. As team members leverage their collective strengths, the organization becomes more adaptable, responsive, and competitive in the market.

Growing Organizations Exponentially

The impact of a high-performance team goes beyond short-term wins. Their growth and cohesion enable organizations to scale quickly and sustainably. As each team member develops their skills, the overall capacity of the organization expands. This cumulative effect leads to faster decision-making, stronger relationships, and greater overall performance. By fostering a high-performance culture, leaders set in motion a cycle of continuous improvement, enabling their organization to thrive in an ever-changing landscape.

Embracing These Principles for Lasting Success

As we look to the future, we must embrace these principles, creating environments where collaboration thrives and high-performance teams flourish. By doing so, we unlock new potentials and build legacies of excellence that inspire future generations. High-performance teams have the power not only to elevate an organization but to drive exponential growth, taking it to new heights and ensuring its long-term success.

Together, we can achieve greatness, transform organizations, and inspire a wave of positive change that will resonate for years to come. In the next chapter, we will discuss how the servant leader converts followers into leaders.

CONVERTING FOLLOWERS INTO LEADERS

INTRODUCTION

Transforming followers into leaders is one of the most complex and demanding tasks that leaders face. In the previous chapter, "The Magic of Teamwork," we explored the tremendous benefits of high-performance teams and examined the essential traits of servant leaders who nurture these teams. However, a critical question remains: Do contemporary leaders possess the skills to transform their followers into influential, tail-end leaders?

In this chapter, we will tackle this question head-on and uncover how you can effectively convert followers into leaders within your organization. Traditional leader-follower dynamics typically concentrate decision-making power solely in the hands of the leader, which can stifle the growth of potential leaders, create inefficiencies, and ultimately hinder team success —especially in the evolving post-COVID-19 workplace.

Eric Hoffer's famous quote, "All leaders strive to turn their followers into children," highlights a leadership approach where leaders feel the need to control every aspect of their followers' actions, maintaining dependency and disengagement. While this might resonate with some leadership styles, it does not reflect the ideals of servant leadership. Too often, leaders unintentionally belittle their followers' potential, creating an environment where growth is stifled and stress levels rise. These counterproductive dynamic places enormous pressure on the leader, leading to burnout and dissatisfaction on both sides.

In contrast, true servant leaders empower their followers. They create an environment where individuals are encouraged to grow, take ownership, and ultimately step into leadership roles themselves. Through guidance, trust, and space for development, servant leaders build a foundation for a team of strong, independent, and capable leaders—ensuring long-term organizational success.

As we progress through this chapter, we will examine the strategies servant leaders use to convert followers into leaders. We will explore the essential shift from command-driven to empowerment-driven leadership and outline practical steps for nurturing leadership qualities within your team. By mastering these principles, you will not only elevate your team's performance but also foster a culture of leadership that will benefit your organization for years to come.

Empowering Followers: The Transformative Power of Servant Leadership

In contrast to traditional leadership, which often seeks to accumulate power and control, servant leadership prioritizes sharing power to nurture the growth and well-being of others. By fostering an environment where followers can grow into leaders themselves, servant leaders create lasting impact. This selfless approach builds strong communities, where leadership is not a personal achievement but a collective, empowering force.

Servant leadership is about more than delegation; it's about unlocking potential. Leaders who understand this truth know that their true influence lies in empowering others to succeed. As highlighted in the article, while followers may be motivated by financial gain, true leaders seek purpose. This deeper motivation fuels passion, sparks innovation, and drives transformational change. By nurturing a sense of purpose, servant leaders develop the next generation of leaders.

John Quincy Adams' words, *"If your actions inspire others to dream more, learn more, do more, and become more, you are a leader,"* encapsulate the essence of servant leadership. Leadership is not about titles but about empowering others to rise and lead. In today's fast-paced, interconnected world, leaders who foster growth, inspire purpose, and nurture potential will create organizations that not only thrive but leave a lasting legacy.

The Perils of Leadership Without Succession: A Fear-Based Legacy

A critical mistake leaders make is failing to nurture successors. Rooted in fear, this oversight stifles growth and sabotages potential. As Aung San Suu Kyi aptly noted, *"It is not power that corrupts but fear. Fear of losing power is what corrupts."* Leaders driven by fear hoard control, preventing others from stepping up, which ultimately undermines their legacy.

This fear manifests in overwork, with leaders shouldering every responsibility. They mistakenly believe that accumulating tasks will ensure their relevance. In reality, this only leads to burnout and inefficiency. Leaders who insist on solving every problem inevitably find themselves overwhelmed, and the control they cherish slips away.

Toxic Leadership

History offers numerous examples of the dangers of unchecked power. Leaders like Adolf Hitler, whose fear-driven need for control led to destruction, demonstrated that leadership without trust and delegation is toxic. In contrast, servant leaders understand that their influence grows by empowering others, not by maintaining sole control.

Leadership without succession planning is a recipe for collapse. When the "go-to" person burns out, chaos ensues. Sustainable leadership isn't about holding power but about creating the conditions for others to rise. Leaders who cultivate successors build enduring legacies. By focusing on succession, leaders ensure that their influence transcends their tenure.

In conclusion, leadership isn't about survival—it's about legacy. True leaders empower others, knowing that their impact is measured by the strength of those who follow. The greatest leaders are those who nurture the potential of others, ensuring that their legacy endures long after they've stepped aside.

The Importance of Succession Planning

In Victor Lipman's *Forbes* article, "Workplace Trend: Stress Is on the Rise," a troubling trend becomes clear—rising stress levels are often the result of poor management and a lack of foresight. Leaders who burn out without preparing successors leave their organizations vulnerable, leading to chaos. As Ralph Nader wisely stated, *"The function of a leader is to produce more leaders, not followers."* This truth strikes at the heart of the leadership crisis today. Indeed, too many leaders, driven by fear or ego, hold on to power and fail to empower the next generation, ultimately doing a disservice to their teams, organizations, and themselves.

As a result, I've witnessed firsthand the difference between a leader who nurtures leaders and one who simply commands followers. The latter is destined for burnout, while the former builds a legacy that endures. Servant-leaders, by contrast, free themselves from the urge to micromanage and prioritize empowerment. By encouraging others to step up, make decisions, and face challenges head-on, servant-leaders cultivate both competence and confidence, instilling a belief in followers that they, too, are capable of leading.

Furthermore, when leaders courageously cultivate leadership in others, they relieve themselves of the crushing burden of doing everything alone. I've seen how organizations transform when decision-making becomes more inclusive. As a result, stress levels decrease, engagement rises, and resilience grows. Followers, freed from fear and submission, begin to operate as if they own the mission, and that makes all the difference.

Therefore, turning followers into leaders is not just a smart strategy—it is essential for organizational longevity. True leadership, after all, is not about control—it's about liberation. It's about creating an environment where individuals feel trusted to make decisions, innovate, and lead with integrity. The most successful organizations, in fact, are those where leadership is shared throughout the ranks—each person a leader, moving the mission forward with confidence and purpose.

In conclusion, this leadership model benefits not only the organization but the leader as well. When leaders groom successors, they ensure the future success of their organizations while liberating themselves from the weight of trying to do it all. Succession planning, therefore, isn't an afterthought; it's the foundation for building a lasting legacy. The servant-leader who turns followers into leaders creates a culture of leadership that thrives long after they step aside. As Proverbs 4:7 reminds us,

"Wisdom is the principal thing; therefore, get wisdom: and with all thy getting get understanding." This wisdom, in leadership, is the key to sustaining growth, both now and in the future.

Delegating Authority: The Cornerstone of Effective Leadership

True leadership thrives on the ability to delegate. Leaders who hoard power and micro-manage erode trust, stifle creativity, and limit the potential of their teams. By delegating authority and entrusting others with the power to act, leaders unlock exceptional results.

A powerful example of this can be found in the story of Pastor Joel Osteen. When he assumed leadership of Lakewood Church during a time of uncertainty, he chose not to tightly control every aspect of the organization. Instead, Osteen empowered others around him to take ownership, trust their instincts, and lead with their strengths. The results were extraordinary: under his guidance, Lakewood Church experienced exponential growth, eventually becoming one of the largest congregations in the world. This success illustrates the power of delegation—when followers are granted autonomy, they rise to the occasion, often exceeding expectations.

Delegating authority is not merely a managerial strategy—it's a courageous act of trust. It communicates confidence in the abilities of those around you, creating a culture of empowerment where innovation and leadership flourish. Leaders who delegate not only lighten their own burdens but foster an environment where collective success becomes possible. This approach is the foundation for long-term growth and sustainability, proving that true leadership is about empowering others, not controlling them.

In essence, effective delegation is the key to leadership that transforms organizations and individuals alike. It's through trusting others with responsibility that leaders build a lasting legacy and achieve greater impact. As John C. Maxwell wisely put it, *"A leader is one who knows the way, goes the way, and shows the way."*

From Command to Empowerment: The Leadership Revolution of David Marquet and the U.S.S. Santa Fe

David Marquet's experience aboard the U.S.S. Santa Fe is a transformative story of leadership that epitomizes servant leadership. It challenges the traditional model of command and control, demonstrating that true leadership lies in empowering others to take ownership and make decisions.

In 1999, Marquet took command of the U.S.S. Santa Fe, a nuclear-powered submarine notorious for its poor performance and disengaged crew. The environment was steeped in a top-down leadership culture where crew members simply followed orders without question. Marquet could have relied on his expertise and continued issuing commands. But a pivotal moment changed his entire approach.

While giving a routine order, Marquet realized that the crew could not carry it out because it was not feasible on their submarine. Despite this, they tried to follow it blindly, a product of their conditioning to never question authority. In that moment, Marquet saw the flaw: the culture had silenced initiative and discouraged independent thinking.

Instead of reinforcing the status quo, Marquet made a radical shift. He decided to empower his crew. Rather than giving orders, he gave authority. His new mantra became, *"Don't ask for permission, tell me what you intend to do."* The crew, once passive followers, now became engaged leaders, taking responsibility and making decisions. They began saying, *"Captain, I intend to..."* signaling their readiness to act.

This simple shift in language transformed the culture. The U.S.S. Santa Fe, once the worst-performing submarine in the fleet, became the best. The crew didn't just follow orders; they became leaders, driven by ownership, trust, and accountability. They were empowered to innovate, solve problems, and take pride in their work.

Marquet's leadership didn't just improve performance; it transformed lives. It's a reminder that leadership is not about holding power but about releasing it—empowering others to rise, think critically, and take responsibility. True leadership isn't about having all the answers; it's about creating an environment where others can lead.

David Marquet's story teaches us that leadership's greatest strength is in lifting others up, empowering them to lead. When we stop giving orders and start empowering others to take responsibility, we create teams that lead with purpose, pride, and passion. This is the essence of servant leadership, and it has the power to transform organizations and the world.

The ERW 12-Point Model for Developing Leaders

1. **Put Your Followers First**: Leadership begins with a commitment to those you serve. Prioritize the growth and well-being of your team, cultivating trust, loyalty, and empowerment. When leaders invest in their followers, they create an environment of collective progress and deep connections.
2. **Integrity**: Integrity is the foundation of trust and respect. As Zig Ziglar said, "Virtue alone won't make you a leader, but you'll never be one without integrity."

Leaders who embody integrity inspire others to uphold the same values, building lasting bonds with their teams.

3. **Forgiveness**: Forgiveness is transformative. As Lewis B. Smedes said, "To forgive is to set a prisoner free and discover that the prisoner was you." Leaders who practice forgiveness create a culture of healing and collaboration, freeing teams from resentment and fostering innovation.
4. **Delegate Authority and Give Control**: Empower your team by giving them the authority to make decisions. As seen in David Marquet's leadership on the U.S.S. Santa Fe, relinquishing control sparks ownership, confidence, and innovation, driving extraordinary growth.
5. **Embrace Diversity**: Diversity fuels creativity and insight. Seek diverse perspectives to navigate complexities and seize opportunities. A diverse team enriches the organization and leads to groundbreaking outcomes.
6. **Foster Open Communication**: Create a space for open dialogue where every voice is valued. Transparency nurtures trust and collaboration, empowering teams to tackle challenges and innovate together.
7. **Invest in Development**: Invest in your team's growth through mentorship and training. When leaders provide opportunities for development, they ignite ambition and belief in their followers' potential, unlocking greater success.
8. **Model Resilience**: In adversity, demonstrate how to rise from setbacks and turn failure into growth. Resilient leaders inspire a growth mindset, teaching their teams to see challenges as opportunities for progress.
9. **Encourage Accountability**: Foster a culture of accountability. When individuals take ownership of

their roles, they drive change and innovation, contributing to shared excellence and organizational success.

10. **Celebrate Successes**: Recognize individual and collective achievements. Celebrating success elevates morale, reinforces positive culture, and motivates teams to keep striving for greatness.
11. **Be Visionary**: Articulate a clear, inspiring vision that resonates with your team. A compelling vision ignites passion and purpose, propelling your team toward a shared mission and direction.
12. **Cultivate Emotional Intelligence**: Develop the ability to understand and manage emotions. Leaders with emotional intelligence create a supportive, empathetic environment, inspiring loyalty, collaboration, and team cohesion.

By embracing these principles, leaders can cultivate a powerful, transformative leadership style that leaves a lasting impact. This model guides leaders toward a legacy of strength, resilience, and unwavering inspiration in an ever-changing world.

Empowering Followers Through Delegation

At the core of servant leadership is empowerment. True servant leaders recognize that micromanagement stifles creativity and breeds resentment. By delegating responsibilities, they trust their teams to take ownership of their work. This act of trust boosts morale and sparks a sense of responsibility, transforming followers into passionate contributors eager to drive results.

Empowering Followers with Clear, Compassionate Communication

Servant leaders excel in communication, delivering a compelling vision that resonates deeply. They engage in meaningful dialogue, ensuring every team member understands how their unique contributions fit into the broader mission. This clarity fosters purpose and motivates full commitment to the team's goals.

Empowering Followers Through Continuous Learning

Servant leaders prioritize growth by cultivating a culture of continuous learning. They provide mentorship, resources, and opportunities for development, empowering their teams to reach their potential. This investment nurtures a resilient, adaptable workforce, ready to face any challenge.

Empowering Followers Through Recognition

Recognition fuels motivation. Servant leaders celebrate both small victories and significant milestones, creating an atmosphere of appreciation. This acknowledgment affirms hard work and dedication, boosting confidence and fostering a strong sense of belonging.

Leading by Example

Servant leaders lead through action. They embody the values they want to instill—integrity, empathy, and commitment—in every interaction. By modeling these behaviors, they inspire their teams to reflect the same principles, fostering a culture of respect and mutual growth.

Fostering Collaboration and Community

Servant leadership thrives on collaboration. Leaders create spaces where diverse voices are heard, transcending hierarchy to nurture innovation. This culture of inclusion empowers teams to share ideas and explore solutions together, driving collective success.

Empowering Followers Through Constructive, Compassionate Feedback

Feedback is a tool for growth, not criticism. Servant leaders offer constructive feedback with empathy, focusing on development. This approach empowers team members to learn from their experiences, encouraging continuous improvement and self-growth.

Empowering Followers by Encouraging Initiative and Creativity

Servant leaders inspire initiative, creating an environment where team members feel free to take risks and propose new ideas. This fosters a culture of creativity, where individuals step outside their comfort zones to drive innovation.

Empowering Followers Through Trust and Consistency

Trust is earned through consistency. Servant leaders build trust by being reliable and transparent. When leaders are authentic and dependable, they create a safe environment for team members to express themselves and collaborate freely.

Empowering Followers by Embracing Failure as Growth

In servant leadership, failure is not the end but a stepping stone. Leaders create a safe space for experimentation, where team members are encouraged to learn from challenges. This mindset drives innovation and resilience, turning setbacks into opportunities for growth.

The Legacy of Servant Leadership

By embracing these principles, servant leaders transform their organizations. They don't just develop followers; they cultivate empowered leaders who are committed to making a difference. This journey of growth and empowerment fosters a future where courage, compassion, and collaboration reign, ensuring that everyone thrives together. In this shared journey, the heart of servant leadership leaves an indelible mark on every individual it touches.

THE EMOTIONAL INTELLIGENCE OF THE SERVANT LEADER: A KEY TOOL FOR TRANSFORMATIVE LEADERSHIP

Emotional intelligence (EI) is the cornerstone of servant leadership, enabling leaders to understand and manage their emotions while empathizing with others. This profound connection fosters an environment of trust, collaboration, and growth. Through EI, servant leaders not only enhance their leadership abilities but also help transform followers into leaders in key areas:

1. Self-Awareness:

Servant leaders recognize their emotional triggers, strengths, and weaknesses, allowing them to lead with authenticity. This self-awareness fosters a culture of openness, encouraging team members to express their feelings and experiences freely. As followers learn to develop their own self-awareness, they gain the clarity to lead themselves and others with greater emotional insight.

2. Empathy:

Empathy is at the heart of servant leadership. By listening actively and validating emotions, servant leaders build trust and create a sense of belonging. When team members feel heard, they become more empathetic themselves, learning to connect with others on a deeper level. This growing empathy enables followers to become leaders who foster compassion and inclusivity within their teams.

3. Emotional Regulation:

Servant leaders manage their emotions effectively, responding thoughtfully rather than reacting impulsively. This composure inspires confidence and stability, helping teams remain resilient during challenging times. Followers who observe this regulation can develop their own emotional control, learning to manage stress and setbacks, and emerging as leaders who guide their teams with calm and clarity.

4. Interpersonal Skills:

Effective communication is a hallmark of emotional intelligence. Servant leaders use emotional insights to tailor their communication, resolving conflicts, addressing concerns, and encouraging collaboration. As followers learn these skills, they become better communicators and relationship-builders, ready to lead their teams with empathy, respect, and understanding.

5. Motivation:

By understanding what drives each individual, servant leaders inspire intrinsic motivation, aligning support with personal goals. This fosters passion and commitment, empowering teams to exceed expectations and contribute to a collective vision. As followers learn to recognize their own sources of motivation, they cultivate the ability to inspire others, becoming leaders who ignite passion and drive in their own teams.

6. Social Awareness:

Servant leaders read social cues and anticipate challenges, creating a harmonious work environment. Their ability to understand team dynamics fosters proactive leadership. Followers who develop this social awareness become leaders who can navigate complex group dynamics, ensuring that every team member feels valued and supported.

7. Conflict Resolution:

Servant leaders approach conflicts with empathy, focusing on underlying emotions. This helps resolve issues constructively and strengthens relationships. As followers absorb these strategies, they develop the ability to mediate and resolve conflicts within their teams, empowering them to lead with fairness and integrity.

8. Fostering a Culture of Emotional Intelligence:

Servant leaders prioritize EI within their teams by modeling behaviors and encouraging emotional skill development. This creates a workplace that values empathy, resilience, and collaboration. As followers learn these skills, they are empowered to cultivate an emotionally intelligent team environment, where everyone thrives and leads.

In conclusion, Emotional Intelligence is the essence of servant leadership. By embodying self-awareness, empathy, emotional regulation, and interpersonal skills, servant leaders not only transform organizations but also help followers grow into leaders themselves. Through EI, servant leaders cultivate a culture of empowerment, where individuals not only thrive but also develop the skills to lead others with compassion, resilience, and vision.

Encouraging Self-Awareness and Even Temperament: Transforming Followers into Servant Leaders

Emotional intelligence (EI) is the cornerstone of servant leadership, with self-awareness as its foundation. Leaders who understand their emotions, recognize their triggers, and manage their reactions set the tone for the entire organization. A leader's emotional state can either inspire or dampen team morale—self-aware leaders foster calm and confidence, cultivating an environment where trust and collaboration thrive.

As David Marquet states, "Leadership is communicating to people their worth and potential so clearly that they are inspired to see it in themselves." Servant leaders who model self-awareness empower followers to transform from passive recipients into active participants in their own growth. By managing internal conflicts with objectivity and embracing vulnerability, leaders create an atmosphere that encourages authenticity and resilience.

Through self-awareness, leaders not only elevate their own leadership but also inspire others to embrace their potential, fostering a culture of continuous development and emotional intelligence that benefits everyone. This transformative leadership ignites collective passion and drives organizational success.

Radiating Positive Energy: Transforming Followers into Leaders

The most profound transformation occurs when leaders radiate positivity, inspiring followers to become leaders themselves. Positive energy is contagious—leaders who exude enthusiasm and optimism cultivate a thriving environment where possibilities flourish. Emotional intelligence plays a key role, as leaders manage their emotions, maintaining an even temperament that fosters trust and encourages followers to take risks and step into leadership roles.

By celebrating achievements and creating a culture of recognition, servant leaders affirm the value of every team member. Followers, empowered and encouraged, begin to see themselves as key contributors, capable of making meaningful decisions. Authentic connections further amplify this transformation, as leaders invest in their followers' growth, nurturing loyalty and commitment.

In this radiant environment, followers emerge as confident leaders, reflecting positive energy back into the organization. This ripple effect drives innovation, collaboration, and collective success, creating a legacy of leadership that empowers future generations to shine brightly.

Transforming Followers into Servant Leaders: Boosting Morale and Engagement

Servant leaders have a unique ability to inspire and uplift their followers, creating a ripple effect of positivity that enhances the entire organization. Unlike traditional bosses who impose authority from afar, effective servant leaders foster environments where individuals feel genuinely valued, supported, and motivated. In contrast, negative leadership breeds stress, disengagement, and stagnation, stifling creativity and undermining morale.

By cultivating a positive atmosphere, servant leaders elevate self-esteem and productivity. This isn't just about maintaining a cheerful facade; it's about celebrating achievements, promoting open communication, and fostering collaboration. When team members feel recognized, their motivation skyrockets, driving them to contribute their best to the collective mission.

As John Maxwell wisely observes, "You don't need to throw titles around to turn your followers into leaders." True leadership transcends hierarchy—it's about empowering others. Servant leaders invest in the growth of their followers, helping them recognize their potential and see themselves as future leaders.

This transformation is powerful. As followers feel uplifted by their leaders' belief in them, they take ownership of their roles, voice ideas, and collaborate more effectively. The result is a dynamic, innovative team that drives success.

In this vibrant environment, morale thrives, and engagement soars. Servant leaders not only elevate spirits but also create a culture of belonging and purpose. When individuals feel connected to their work and each other, they go above and beyond, fostering excellence across the organization.

Ultimately, servant leaders leave a lasting legacy—an empowered, thriving organization where everyone has the opportunity to grow, lead, and succeed.

KEY SKILLS, TECHNIQUES, AND VIRTUES TO TRANSFORM FOLLOWERS INTO LEADERS

Transforming followers into leaders is about more than delegation; it's about nurturing essential skills and virtues that inspire individuals to reach their full potential. As a servant leader, your role is to create an environment that encourages growth and empowers others to become effective leaders.

1. **Empathy as a Foundation**: Start with empathy. Encourage followers to understand the feelings and perspectives of others, fostering trust and collaboration. By modeling empathy, you create a culture where everyone feels valued, laying the foundation for authentic leadership.
2. **Communication Skills**: Teach the art of communication—articulating ideas clearly and listening actively. Communication builds bridges between people. By encouraging open dialogues, you create a respectful environment where ideas flow freely, strengthening relationships and understanding.
3. **Problem-Solving Techniques**: Instill critical thinking and problem-solving skills. Challenge followers to analyze situations and find creative solutions. This

approach builds their confidence and prepares them to turn challenges into opportunities.

4. **Integrity and Accountability**: Emphasize integrity and accountability. Teach followers that leadership requires owning not only their actions but also their impact on others. A leader's integrity builds trust and respect, which are the cornerstones of effective leadership.
5. **Vision Creation**: Encourage followers to develop their own vision for success. A clear vision drives passion and purpose. Help them articulate their aspirations and align them with the organization's goals, ensuring they see their role in the bigger picture.
6. **Resilience Building**: Equip followers with tools to handle adversity. Teach them to view setbacks as stepping stones to success, helping them navigate challenges with confidence and grace. Resilience strengthens leaders, enabling them to rise stronger from difficulties.
7. **Fostering Teamwork**: Teach the value of collaboration. Leadership thrives in teams, not in isolation. Encourage followers to appreciate diverse perspectives, work collectively, and celebrate shared success, cultivating a more inclusive and supportive environment.
8. **Continuous Learning**: Instill a mindset of lifelong learning. Encourage curiosity, feedback, and development. Great leaders never stop growing, and by modeling this behavior, you inspire followers to pursue their growth relentlessly.
9. **Positive Reinforcement**: Use positive reinforcement to boost morale and encourage growth. Celebrate achievements, no matter how small. Recognition uplifts spirit and reinforces the behaviors you want to cultivate, creating a cycle of motivation and engagement.

10. **Leading by Example**: The most powerful teaching tool is your example. Live out the virtues you wish to instill. Your actions, grounded in authenticity and compassion, will resonate more deeply than any lecture. By embodying servant leadership, you set a standard that others will strive to emulate.

By integrating these skills, techniques, and virtues into your leadership, you create an environment where followers can flourish into influential leaders. This commitment to development not only elevates individuals but enriches the entire organization, fostering a culture of empowerment, collaboration, and shared success.

FOSTERING A POSITIVE COMPANY CULTURE AS A SERVANT LEADER

As a servant leader, cultivating a positive company culture is one of the most powerful ways to drive employee satisfaction, boost morale, and enhance productivity. A thriving culture doesn't just happen—it requires intentional actions that align with core values. Here's how you can foster an environment that inspires your team:

1. Lead with Empathy

Empathy creates trust and deepens connections. As Brené Brown says, *"Empathy has no script. There is no right way or wrong way to do it. It's simply listening, holding space, withholding judgment, emotionally connecting, and communicating that incredibly healing message of 'You're not alone.'"* When employees feel understood, they flourish. Begin by understanding the needs and concerns of your team. Show genuine care for their well-being, both personally and professionally. As Maya Angelou wisely said, *"People will forget what you said, people will forget what you did, but people will never forget how you made them feel."* Empathy builds trust and makes employees feel valued and heard.

2. Encourage Open Communication

Create an open-door policy that invites team members to share ideas freely. Peter Drucker wisely stated, *"The most important thing in communication is hearing what isn't said."* Regular opportunities for dialogue, such as team meetings and feedback sessions, cultivate an environment where all voices are heard. Proverbs 15:23 reminds us, *"A person finds joy in giving an apt reply—and how good is a timely word!"* Open communication fosters mutual respect and understanding.

3. Recognize and Celebrate Achievements

As William James observed, *"The deepest principle in human nature is the craving to be appreciated."* Regularly acknowledge both individual and team successes, no matter how small. Celebrating achievements fosters a sense of belonging and reinforces the idea that everyone's contributions are vital to the organization's success. As Hebrews 10:24 says, *"And let us consider how we may spur one another on toward love and good deeds."* The verse encourages team members to actively think about ways to inspire and motivate one another. Recognition creates a culture of appreciation and motivation.

4. Promote Work-Life Balance

Encourage a healthy balance between work and personal life. Leaders who respect boundaries inspire loyalty and engagement. Arianna Huffington reminds us, *"We think, mistakenly, that success is the result of the amount of time we put in at work, instead of the quality of time we put in."* When well-being is prioritized, productivity naturally follows.

5. Foster Inclusivity and Diversity

Create a culture that values diversity in all forms. Embrace different perspectives and experiences, ensuring everyone feels included and appreciated. Diversity not only enriches the workplace but fuels creativity and innovation. 1 Corinthians 12:14 reminds us, *"Even so the body is not made up of one part but of many."* Every individual contributes uniquely to the collective strength of the team.

6. Empower Your Team

Delegate authority and give employees the autonomy to lead. Empowerment builds confidence and inspires accountability. John Quincy Adams captured this idea perfectly: *"If your actions inspire others to dream more, learn more, do more, and become more, you are a leader."* Trusting your team elevates their potential.

7. Invest in Development

Encourage continuous learning and growth. Provide opportunities for training, mentorship, and skill development. When employees see that you are committed to their future, they are more likely to invest their energy into the organization. Proverbs 1:5 encourages, *"Let the wise listen and add to their learning, and let the discerning get guidance."* Growth is a journey, and leaders who invest in development create a cycle of continuous improvement.

8. Create a Safe Environment

Encourage a culture of psychological safety where risks can be taken without fear. Innovation flourishes when failure is seen as a learning opportunity. As Nelson Mandela noted, *"I never lose. I either win or learn."* A safe and supportive space encourages creativity and resilience. A safe environment empowers your team to flourish without fear.

9. Model Positive Behavior

Live out the values and behaviors you wish to see in your team. Your actions, work ethic, and interactions set the tone for the organization. As Colossians 3:23 says, *"Whatever you do, work at it with all your heart, as working for the Lord, not for human masters."* Positivity is contagious; when you lead with integrity and joy, others will follow suit.

10. Solicit Feedback and Adapt

Regularly seek feedback from your team about workplace culture and areas for improvement. Be open to making changes based on their insights. This adaptability shows that you value their input and are committed to creating a positive environment. James 1:5 encourages, *"If any of you lacks wisdom, let him ask of God, who gives to all liberally and without reproach, and it will be given to him."* Continual improvement stems from a willingness to listen and grow.

By implementing these strategies, you can cultivate a company culture grounded in empathy, inclusivity, and recognition. A servant leader's commitment to creating such an environment not only enhances employee satisfaction but drives organizational success, leaving a lasting impact on both individuals and the entire organization. As Proverbs 11:25 says, *"A generous person will prosper; whoever refreshes others will be refreshed."* When you uplift others, you create an atmosphere where everyone can thrive.

LEADING BY EXAMPLE: KEY TO TRANSFORMING FOLLOWERS INTO LEADERS

Leading by example is the cornerstone of cultivating future leaders. Your actions set the standard, inspiring and empowering others to rise to their potential. Here are 10 key focal points to help you set the proper standards:

1. **Live Core Values**: Consistently demonstrate integrity, respect, and transparency. When your team sees you embody these values, they are more likely to follow suit.
2. **Practice Accountability**: Own your mistakes and decisions. This openness fosters a culture of responsibility and trust.
3. **Exhibit Work Ethic**: Show dedication and excellence in your work. Your commitment inspires others to strive for the same.
4. **Demonstrate Emotional Intelligence**: Engage empathetically with your team. Model understanding and self-awareness to teach the importance of managing emotions effectively.
5. **Encourage Growth**: Share your learning journey and support professional development. This sets the tone for continuous improvement.
6. **Welcome Feedback**: Seek input and show you value others' perspectives. This builds trust and encourages open dialogue.
7. **Celebrate Success**: Highlight team achievements to reinforce that leadership is about uplifting others.
8. **Show Resilience**: Navigate challenges with composure and determination, inspiring your team to view setbacks as opportunities.
9. **Foster Collaboration**: Work alongside your team, emphasizing shared goals and collective success.
10. **Stay Vision-Focused**: Communicate and commit to your vision, inspiring alignment, and purpose across the organization.

By leading with authenticity and purpose, you empower your followers to become leaders themselves. This ripple effect builds a culture of growth, trust, and collaboration, driving organizational success and impact.

MODEL DESIRED BEHAVIORS AND STAY COMMITTED IN YOUR QUEST TO CONVERT YOUR FOLLOWERS TO LEADERS

In the journey of transforming followers into leaders, effective leadership hinges on the powerful principle of modeling desired behaviors. It's not merely about instructing others but demonstrating the qualities and actions you wish to see in them. Here's how to commit to this transformative process:

1. **Engage Actively**: Step into the trenches alongside your team. When you work alongside them, sharing both the challenges and triumphs, you cultivate a sense of unity and purpose. Your hands-on involvement shows that you value their contributions and are invested in the collective success of the group.

2. **Fulfill Promises**: Trust is the foundation of effective leadership. When you make commitments, honor them diligently. By consistently delivering on your promises, you establish a culture of reliability and integrity, encouraging your followers to do the same.

3. **Exemplify Integrity**: Your moral compass should guide every decision you make. Uphold high ethical standards and be transparent in your actions. As Billy J. Grogan wisely states, "Great leaders are great followers, and great followers become great leaders." Your integrity sets a powerful precedent, inspiring your followers to embody the same principles in their actions.

4. **Demonstrate Accountability**: When challenges arise or mistakes are made, own up to them openly. This practice not only humanizes you but also creates an environment where your followers feel safe to take risks and learn from their own missteps. By showing that accountability is a strength, you empower them to adopt this vital trait.

5. **Maintain High Standards**: Strive for excellence in every task and interaction. Your commitment to quality and continuous improvement sets a benchmark for your team. When they see you pushing for the best outcomes, they will be inspired to elevate their own performance and take pride in their work.

6. **Encourage Open Communication**: Foster an environment where dialogue is encouraged. When you actively listen to your team's ideas, concerns, and feedback, you model respect and value for their perspectives. This practice empowers them to express themselves freely, cultivating a culture of collaboration.

7. **Celebrate Efforts and Achievements**: Recognize and celebrate both small wins and significant achievements. By acknowledging the hard work of your team, you not only boost morale but also reinforce the behaviors and attitudes you want to cultivate. This celebration of effort motivates them to strive for greater heights.

8. **Demonstrate Resilience**: Show how you navigate obstacles with determination and grace. Your ability to remain composed under pressure teaches your followers the importance of resilience. When they

witness your steadfastness, it encourages them to adopt a similar mindset in their own challenges.

9. **Share Your Vision**: Clearly articulate your vision and the values that drive your leadership. By consistently communicating your goals and aspirations, you inspire your followers to align their efforts with a greater purpose. This clarity fosters a shared sense of direction and commitment.

10. **Be a Lifelong Learner**: Embrace your own journey of growth and learning. Share your experiences, insights, and the lessons you've learned along the way. By modeling a commitment to self-improvement, you encourage your followers to pursue their own paths of development and embrace lifelong learning.

In essence, by modeling desired behaviors and staying committed to your values, you create a fertile ground for leadership development within your team. Your actions set the tone, inspiring followers to step into their potential and emerge as leaders in their own right. This transformative process not only strengthens individual capabilities but also enriches the collective spirit of your organization, paving the way for sustained success and innovation.

APPROACHABILITY AND RELATABILITY: CONNECT WITH YOUR FOLLOWERS

In the realm of effective leadership, approachability and relatability are not just desirable traits—they are essential. When leaders cultivate a warm and open demeanor, they create an environment where followers feel valued and empowered. Here's how to foster genuine connections with your team:

1. **Be Present**: Make a conscious effort to be available and engaged. Whether through regular check-ins, open-door policies, or informal gatherings, your presence signals that you care about your followers as individuals, not just as employees.

2. **Listen Actively**: Show genuine interest in what your team has to say. Practice active listening by giving your full attention, asking clarifying questions, and acknowledging their thoughts and feelings. This not only fosters trust but also encourages them to share openly.

3. **Share Your Story**: Relatability flourishes when leaders are willing to be vulnerable. Share your experiences, challenges, and lessons learned. This openness not only humanizes you but also invites your followers to connect on a deeper level, making them more willing to engage and share their own stories.

4. **Acknowledge Individuality**: Recognize and celebrate the unique strengths and perspectives each team member brings.

Tailor your approach to suit their personalities and communication styles. By valuing diversity, you cultivate a sense of belonging and appreciation within the team.

1. **Encourage Dialogue**: Create opportunities for open conversations where team members feel comfortable sharing their ideas, concerns, and feedback. Facilitate discussions that encourage collaboration and creativity, allowing everyone to contribute to the collective vision.

2. **Be Approachable in Conflict**: When tensions arise, approach conflicts with empathy and understanding. Be willing to address issues head-on while maintaining a calm demeanor. This approach fosters an atmosphere of trust and shows that you value resolution over authority.

3. **Offer Support and Encouragement**: Regularly check in on your followers' well-being. Offer support during challenging times and celebrate their successes. Your genuine concern for their personal and professional growth strengthens the bond between you and your team or organization.

4. **Facilitate Team Building**: Organize team-building activities that promote connection and camaraderie. These informal settings allow team members to bond outside of their usual roles, fostering stronger relationships and enhancing collaboration.

5. **Solicit Feedback**: Actively seek input from your team on decisions and initiatives. When followers feel their opinions matter, they are more likely to invest themselves in the outcomes, transitioning from passive participants to proactive contributors.

6. **Practice Gratitude**: Regularly express appreciation for your team's hard work and dedication. A simple "thank you" can go a long way in reinforcing a positive culture and showing your followers that their efforts are recognized and valued.

By embracing approachability and relatability, you transform your leadership from a position of authority to one of partnership and collaboration. This relational dynamic not only prevents disengagement but also ignites a sense of ownership and commitment among your followers. When team members feel seen, heard, and valued, they are inspired to contribute actively, fueling a culture of trust, innovation, and collective success. Ultimately, these connections pave the way for a thriving organization where every individual is empowered to rise as a leader in their own right.

FOSTER COLLABORATIVE ENVIRONMENTS: A PATH TO TRANSFORMING FOLLOWERS INTO LEADERS

In today's dynamic workplace, fostering a collaborative environment is essential, especially for Generation X, Generation Z, and millennials—who thrive on teamwork and connection—who make up a significant portion of the workforce. By promoting a culture of collaboration, you not only empower your followers but also pave the way for their transformation into effective leaders. He is ten vital skills to help you cultivate this vital environment:

1. **Encourage Open Communication**: Create channels for open dialogue where team members can share ideas, feedback, and concerns without fear of judgment. This openness nurtures trust and fosters an atmosphere where collaboration can flourish.

2. **Emphasize Team Goals**: Align individual objectives with team goals to promote a sense of shared purpose. When followers see how their contributions impact the larger mission, they become more invested in the team's success, cultivating a leadership mindset.

3. **Celebrate Diversity of Thought**: Recognize that each team member brings unique perspectives and skills to the table. Encourage brainstorming sessions where all ideas are valued, fostering innovation and creative problem-solving. This diversity enriches the collaborative process and enhances collective decision-making.

4. **Facilitate Cross-Functional Projects**: Encourage collaboration across different departments to break down silos. By working together on cross-functional projects, team members gain a broader understanding of the organization, enhancing their leadership skills and fostering interdepartmental relationships.

5. **Create Safe Spaces for Collaboration**: Develop spaces —both physical and virtual—where team members can come together to collaborate freely. These environments should promote comfort and creativity, allowing individuals to share ideas without hesitation.

6. **Encourage Peer-to-Peer Learning**: Implement mentorship programs or peer-learning initiatives where team members can share expertise and insights. This not only enhances individual skills but also strengthens bonds and encourages a culture of mutual support.

7. **Empower Decision-Making**: Delegate authority by allowing teams to make decisions collaboratively. This empowerment instills a sense of ownership and responsibility, enabling followers to take initiative and act as leaders within the group.

8. **Promote Accountability**: Foster a culture where team members hold each other accountable for their contributions. This collective responsibility reinforces commitment and encourages individuals to step up and lead by example.

9. **Reward Collaboration**: Recognize and celebrate collaborative efforts and team successes. By acknowledging collective achievements, you reinforce the value of teamwork and encourage others to engage in cooperative behaviors.

10. **Model Collaborative Leadership**: As a leader, demonstrate collaborative behaviors by actively participating in discussions, valuing input from all team members, and showing a willingness to compromise. Your actions set the tone for the team and inspire followers to adopt a similar approach.

By fostering a collaborative environment, you not only enhance engagement and productivity but also cultivate the next generation of leaders. As Walt Disney wisely stated, "Whatever we accomplish belongs to our entire group, a tribute to our combined efforts." When your followers feel empowered to work together, share their voices, and contribute to a common vision, they develop the skills, confidence, and mindset necessary to lead. In this environment of shared success, every team member becomes a leader in their own right, driving the organization forward and achieving remarkable results together.

EMPOWERING YOUR FOLLOWERS THROUGH CONTINUOUS DEVELOPMENT

In the ever-evolving landscape of leadership, the commitment to life-long learning is paramount. Great leaders understand that the pursuit of knowledge never ends; it is a journey that enriches both personal growth and organizational success. Icons like Warren Buffett and Bill Gates exemplify this dedication, spending substantial time reading and seeking new insights. By fostering a culture of continuous learning, you empower your followers to thrive and innovate.

1. **Model a Growth Mindset**: Demonstrate your own commitment to learning by sharing your experiences and insights. Show your followers that it's okay to ask questions, seek feedback, and explore new ideas. Your openness to growth inspires them to adopt a similar mindset.

2. **Encourage Curiosity**: Create an environment where curiosity is celebrated. Encourage your team to explore new topics, ask questions, and pursue interests that expand their horizons. This curiosity fosters creativity and adaptability, essential traits in today's fast-paced world.

3. **Provide Learning Opportunities**: Invest in professional development by offering workshops, training sessions, and access to online courses. By providing resources and opportunities, you signal that continuous learning is valued and supported within the organization.

4. **Facilitate Knowledge Sharing**: Create platforms—such as lunch-and-learns or team discussions—where team members can share insights and lessons learned from their experiences. This collaboration enhances collective knowledge and reinforces the idea that learning is a shared responsibility.

5. **Recognize Achievements**: Celebrate instances of growth and learning within your team. Whether someone completes a course or shares a new perspective, acknowledgment fosters a positive culture of learning and motivates others to pursue their own development.

6. **Encourage Mentorship**: Pair experienced team members with those seeking growth through mentoring relationships. These partnerships provide a space for knowledge exchange and personal development, empowering followers to learn from one another.

7. **Embrace Failure as a Learning Tool**: Shift the narrative around failure from a negative experience to a valuable learning opportunity. Encourage your team to reflect on setbacks and extract lessons that contribute to their growth and resilience.

8. **Promote External Learning**: Encourage attendance at conferences, webinars, and industry events. Engaging with external thought leaders and innovators broadens perspectives and fosters new ideas that can be brought back to the team.

9. **Set Learning Goals**: Challenge your followers to set personal learning objectives that align with their career

aspirations. This proactive approach to learning empowers them to take ownership of their development.

10. **Incorporate Feedback Loops**: Establish a regular feedback mechanism that encourages open dialogue about growth areas and opportunities for development. This not only enhances individual performance but also fosters a culture of continuous improvement.

By committing to lifelong learning, you empower your followers to realize their full potential. As John F. Kennedy wisely stated, "Leadership and learning are indispensable to each other." In nurturing a culture where learning is embedded in the fabric of your organization, you not only cultivate capable leaders but also create a thriving environment where innovation and resilience flourish. Your followers will emerge as empowered leaders, equipped with the knowledge and skills to navigate challenges and seize opportunities in an ever-changing world.

SUMMARY: THE ERW 12 POINT MODEL FOR TRANSFORMING FOLLOWERS INTO LEADERS

1. **Prioritize Your Followers**: At the heart of effective leadership lies a profound commitment to those you lead. By placing your followers' needs above mere profits, you cultivate an environment of loyalty and trust. This dedication ignites their passion and unleashes their potential, allowing them to give their best efforts and create remarkable results.

2. **Instill Integrity**: Integrity is the bedrock of leadership. It is the unwavering commitment to honesty and ethical behavior that earns respect and builds credibility. By instilling this value in your followers, you empower them to act with conviction and create a culture where trust flourishes. As you model integrity, you inspire others to uphold these principles, fostering a community built on honor and accountability.

3. **Promote Forgiveness**: In a world rife with challenges, the ability to forgive is transformative. Encourage a culture where understanding and compassion reign. When followers feel safe to forgive and let go of grievances, they foster resilience and collaboration, creating an atmosphere ripe for innovation. This powerful practice not only heals wounds but propels your team forward.

4. **Delegate Authority**: True leadership is not about control; it's about empowerment. By delegating authority, you give your followers the power to make decisions and take ownership of their work. This trust transforms them into capable leaders, igniting their drive and creativity. When people feel they have a stake in the outcome, their commitment deepens, leading to extraordinary achievements.

5. **Foster Emotional Intelligence**: Emotional intelligence is a vital skill for effective leadership. Encourage your followers to cultivate self-awareness and manage their emotions. This understanding enables them to navigate challenges with grace and poise, creating a harmonious workplace. Leaders who practice emotional intelligence inspire others to connect deeply and communicate

authentically, fostering a culture of empathy and support.

6. **Radiate Positive Energy**: The energy you bring to your leadership role can elevate your entire team. By radiating positivity and enthusiasm, you create an environment that motivates and inspires. This uplifting atmosphere boosts morale, enhances creativity, and encourages your followers to embrace challenges with a renewed sense of vigor. As you shine brightly, you illuminate the path for others to follow.

7. **Instill Key Virtues**: Cultivating essential virtues—humility, empathy, patience, tolerance, fairness, and courage—shapes the character of your followers. These qualities are the foundation of effective leadership. When you actively promote these virtues, you empower your team to lead with heart and integrity, fostering a culture where everyone thrives.

8. **Cultivate a Positive Culture**: A positive organizational culture is a powerful catalyst for success. Emphasize respect, inclusivity, and transparency to build strong relationships. When your followers feel valued and heard, they are more engaged and motivated to contribute. This sense of belonging transforms a group of individuals into a cohesive unit, working towards a shared vision.

9. **Lead by Example**: Actions speak louder than words. By modeling the behaviors and attitudes you wish to see in your followers, you set a powerful standard. Your commitment to excellence, resilience, and ethical behavior inspires others to rise to the occasion. When

leaders walk the talk, they create a ripple effect of positive change.

10. **Be Approachable**: True leadership is not about maintaining distance; it's about connection. By being approachable and relatable, you foster open communication and build trust. When followers feel comfortable sharing their thoughts and concerns, they become active contributors rather than passive participants. This connection enhances collaboration and drives collective success.

11. **Encourage Team Spirit**: In a world that often celebrates individual achievement, fostering a spirit of teamwork is essential. Promote collaboration and transparency, emphasizing that collective success is built on shared efforts. When your followers understand the value of working together, they become a formidable force, ready to tackle any challenge that comes their way.

12. **Commit to Lifelong Learning**: The journey of leadership is one of continuous growth. Great leaders are insatiably curious, always seeking knowledge and new perspectives. By promoting a culture of lifelong learning, you inspire your followers to embrace their own development. As they grow, so does your organization, leading to innovation and adaptability in an ever-changing world.

The path from follower to leader begins with mastering the art of following. Aristotle's insight, *"He who cannot be a good follower cannot be a good leader,"* underscores that leadership starts with humility and learning. Effective leadership is not solitary but a shared journey rooted in servant leadership—uplifting others, fostering growth, and building trust.

"Leadership is not about being in charge but taking care of those in your charge," says Simon Sinek. By embodying courage, compassion, and positivity, leaders inspire resilience and transform followers into passionate, self-driven leaders. Collaboration and open communication are key to creating empowered teams and dynamic organizations.

Leadership is a continuous evolution of shared values and lifelong learning. Ralph Nader reminds us, *"The function of leadership is to produce more leaders, not more followers."* Let us lead with purpose, inspiring others to rise and create a legacy of empowerment. In the words of John Quincy Adams, *"If your actions inspire others to dream more, learn more, do more, and become more, you are a leader."*

THE ESSENTIALS OF TIME MANAGEMENT

INTRODUCTION

Time is arguably the most precious resource bestowed upon humanity. As life progresses, many people, particularly those nearing its end, often express a desire for more time rather than more money. This sentiment echoes the wisdom found in Colossians 4:5: "Walk in wisdom toward outsiders, making the best use of the time."

In this chapter, we will equip you with transformative strategies, practical tips, and essential tools to manage your time effectively. We'll delve into identifying time-robbers and time-wasters, ensuring you can distinguish between mere busyness and genuine productivity. By implementing these principles, you can enhance your effectiveness both at work and home, ultimately enabling you to spend quality time with loved ones. Additionally, we will explore common time management pitfalls and how to avoid them.

Mankind's Quest for Time

Humanity's relentless preoccupation with time has fueled a remarkable journey of innovation and progress, as we strive to manage and optimize this most precious resource. Consider the dramatic transformation in travel: a journey from New York to California that once took 40 arduous days on foot can now be completed in just 5 hours and 20 minutes by air. This leap forward epitomizes a monumental achievement in time management.

Technological advancements have further reshaped our relationship with time. Innovations like artificial intelligence, electronic fax, and email have not only accelerated communication but have also altered the very fabric of our work and personal lives. As Psalm 90:12 poignantly reminds us, "Teach us to number our days that we may gain a heart of wisdom." This ancient wisdom underscores the urgency of mastering our time, as it is a finite resource.

Time is invaluable, and once lost, it cannot be regained. As Tony Robbins aptly stated, "When a person only has two minutes to live, no amount of money in the world can increase those minutes." This profound truth illuminates the necessity of effective time management for anyone aiming to excel professionally, lead effectively, or cultivate a fulfilling personal life.

Research consistently shows that effective time management correlates with higher job satisfaction, career advancement, personal growth, and even wealth creation. By learning to prioritize, delegate, and focus on what truly matters, individuals enhance their productivity and enrich their lives and relationships.

In this quest for mastery over time, we discover that the journey itself can be as valuable as the destination. As we navigate the complexities of modern life, let us remember that how we choose to spend our time shapes our experiences, influences our legacies, and ultimately defines the essence of our existence.

COMMON TIME MANAGEMENT MISTAKES

Mistake #1: Perfectionism

While striving for quality work is admirable, chasing perfection is often a fool's errand. The relentless pursuit of perfection can lead to stress and frustration—not just for you, but for those around you. Embrace the idea that "done is better than perfect." Perfectionism can stifle productivity and hinder progress.

Mistake #2: Having a Vague or No Purpose

A lack of clear vision or purpose is a major time management pitfall. Without a well-defined goal, you risk confusion and aimlessness. As a servant leader, it's essential to articulate a singular vision, revisit it regularly, and align your actions with that purpose to ensure meaningful results.

Mistake #3: Not Getting Rid of Distractions

Distractions are among the most significant barriers to effective time management. Social media, constant email checks, and unnecessary conversations can easily derail your focus. To manage your time wisely, identify and eliminate these distractions to create a more conducive work environment.

Mistake #4: Poor Planning Skills

Failing to plan effectively or set clear priorities can scatter your efforts and waste valuable time. A lack of preparation is a time management killer. Take the time to plan your day meticulously, prioritize your tasks, and avoid rushing through them—this can prevent mistakes that lead to rework and frustration.

Mistake #5: Not Understanding the Difference Between Being Busy and Being Effective

Busyness does not equate to productivity. Many individuals conflate the two, focusing on appearing busy rather than achieving meaningful results. As a servant leader, prioritize effectiveness and clarity over mere activity. Recognize what truly matters to maintain energy and motivation.

Mistake #6: Multitasking

Multitasking may seem efficient, but it often diminishes productivity and increases errors. Concentrating on one task at a time allows for greater quality and effectiveness. Addressing multitasking habits is essential for enhancing your overall time management skills.

Mistake #7: Saying Yes Too Often

Overcommitting by saying yes to every request can lead to chaos and burnout. Learning to say no is a vital skill for effective time management. Evaluate each request carefully, only committing to what aligns with your goals and capacity without sacrificing your well-being.

Mistake #8: No Accurate Understanding of What Is Essential

Failing to identify what is essential can severely hinder your progress. Study successful practices, learn from others, and focus on the tasks that truly matter. Prioritizing essential activities will streamline your path to achieving your goals.

Mistake #9: Failing to Delegate or Outsource

Attempting to do everything yourself is a common error in time management. Delegating and outsourcing tasks where appropriate. enhances efficiency and effectiveness. Trusting others to handle responsibilities allows you to focus on your strengths, avoiding burnout and ineffectiveness.

Mistake #10: Overcommitment and Taking on Too Much

Taking on too many responsibilities can overwhelm you and diminish your productivity. It's crucial to manage your workload judiciously and avoid biting off more than you can chew. As a servant leader, aim to under promise and overdeliver, maintaining control over your commitments while safeguarding your time and energy.

By recognizing and addressing these common time management mistakes, you can cultivate a more effective, fulfilling approach to both your professional and personal life. Embracing these lessons can transform your relationship with time, leading to enhanced productivity and deeper connections with those around you.

Busy People Versus Productive People – The Servant Leader's Advice

Benjamin Franklin wisely noted, "If you want something done, ask a busy person." Indeed, busy individuals often seem to accomplish more simply because they don't waste time. Yet, it's crucial to recognize that busyness does not always translate to productivity.

Advice: Stay busy, but prioritize producing tangible results. The synergy of being both busy and productive can dramatically transform your life.

Busy yet nonproductive individuals frequently take on more tasks while current ones languish unfinished. In contrast, productive individuals are discerning before agreeing to additional commitments, mastering the art of saying no when necessary. They recognize their limitations and focus on their primary goals, ensuring their energy is channeled effectively.

Moreover, busy, nonproductive people often fall into the trap of multitasking—juggling various priorities that ultimately lead to increased stress and decreased quality of work. In stark contrast, productive people emphasize deep work, concentrating on one critical task at a time. Research shows that multitasking is a myth; it fragments attention and diminishes overall productivity.

The workspace of busy, nonproductive individuals tends to reflect their chaotic approach.

Additionally, while busy people may frequently vocalize their hectic schedules, productive individuals let their results speak volumes. Busyness often equates to a frantic approach, while productivity embodies a strategic mindset. The former may lead to being seen as proficient in many tasks, but the latter focuses on excellence in a select few.

Productive individuals aim to accomplish at least one meaningful task each day, surrounding themselves with supporters who uplift and inspire them. They recognize that the journey of productivity is not just about doing more, but about achieving more with intent and clarity.

In summary, as a servant leader, cultivate a culture that values meaningful productivity over mere busyness. Encourage your team to focus on impactful work, prioritize critical tasks, and celebrate the achievement of significant results. By doing so, you empower them to move beyond the chaos of busyness and into the realm of true productivity.

USING TECHNOLOGY TO MANAGE TIME – THE SERVANT LEADER'S APPROACH

In today's fast-paced digital landscape, technology can serve as a formidable ally in mastering time management. For servant leaders, leveraging these tools not only enhances personal productivity but also empowers team members to work more efficiently.

Here's a closer look at some essential tools that can transform how you and your team manage time:

1. **Google Calendar**: This versatile tool is invaluable for scheduling meetings and deadlines. By syncing with various third-party applications, it creates a seamless interface for managing personal and professional commitments. Encourage your team to share calendars, fostering transparency and collaboration in scheduling.

2. **Rescue Time**: Understanding how time is spent is crucial for improvement. Rescue Time is a powerful tool for enhancing productivity by tracking how time is spent across apps, websites, and tasks. It generates detailed reports categorizing activities as productive or distracting, helping users identify inefficiencies. With these insights, individuals or teams can set productivity goals, block distractions using the "Focus Time" feature, and develop strategies for more focused work. Sharing reports fosters transparency and collaboration, enabling teams to address inefficiencies collectively.

3. **Remember The Milk**: This advanced to-do list app not only integrates with Google Calendar but also offers robust project management features. As a servant

leader, you can use this tool to delegate tasks effectively, ensuring everyone knows their responsibilities while maintaining accountability.

4. **Pomodoro Technique**: This time management method encourages breaking work into 25-minute focused intervals, followed by short breaks. By promoting the Pomodoro Technique within your team, you create a rhythm of productivity that helps reduce burnout and sustain engagement, making work feel more manageable. https:// pomofocus.io

5. **Taoist**: With its comprehensive task organization capabilities, Taoist allows individuals to capture and prioritize tasks efficiently. Emphasize the importance of maintaining a clear task list, and encourage your team to utilize this tool to focus on what truly matters each day. https://todoist.com

6. **Focus Keeper**: To combat anxiety related to time pressures, Focus Keeper enhances concentration by setting clear work intervals. This tool can be particularly beneficial during high-stress projects, providing a structured way to stay on track without feeling overwhelmed. https://focuskeeper.co

The Servant Leader's Commitment

As a servant leader, your role is not only to implement these tools but also to model their use. Share your own strategies for leveraging technology effectively, and encourage your team to explore these options. Foster an environment where everyone feels empowered to seek out and utilize the tools that resonate with them, promoting a culture of continuous improvement.

By integrating technology into your time management approach, you enhance not only your own effectiveness but also that of your entire team. Remember, the ultimate goal is to cultivate a workspace where everyone feels equipped to manage their time wisely, leading to greater productivity, satisfaction, and overall success.

COMMON TIME WASTERS – THE SERVANT LEADER'S ADVICE

Victor Hugo wisely noted, "Short as life is, we make it still shorter by the careless waste of time." As servant leaders, it's crucial to identify and mitigate common time wasters that can hinder personal and team productivity. Here's a guide to avoid these pitfalls:

1. **Ineffective Scheduling**: Understanding your own peak productivity times is essential. Schedule high-concentration tasks during your most energetic periods, whether that's early in the morning or late afternoon. Encourage your team to do the same, promoting a culture that values productivity over mere busyness.

2. **Denying Time Management Issues**: Acknowledging the need for better time management is the first step toward improvement. Complaining about a lack of time doesn't create more time; it only highlights the need for strategic change. Foster an environment where team members feel safe to discuss their challenges openly, allowing for collective problem-solving.

3. **Neglecting Daily Planning**: Without a clear plan, each day can quickly devolve into chaos. Encourage your team to spend a few minutes each morning setting goals

and priorities. This simple practice can dramatically enhance efficiency, making it easier to stay focused on what truly matters.

4. **Allowing Urgent Tasks to Overtake Important Ones**: It's easy to get caught up in the whirlwind of urgent tasks, but distinguishing between urgent and important is vital. Teach your team to prioritize effectively and encourage them to delegate or schedule urgent tasks when they don't align with their primary goals. This practice helps maintain focus on what drives long-term success.

5. **Being Rigid and Inflexible**: Life is unpredictable, and a rigid schedule can lead to frustration. Promote flexibility within your team's calendars to accommodate unexpected interruptions or opportunities. Encourage a mindset that views adaptability as a strength, ensuring that your team can pivot, when necessary, without losing sight of their objectives.

6. **Excessive Meetings**: Meetings can drain valuable time if not managed properly. Encourage setting clear agendas, keeping meetings concise, and inviting only those who need to be present. Consider alternative methods for communication, like emails or collaborative platforms, to reduce the number of unnecessary meetings.

7. **Poor Communication**: Misunderstandings and unclear directives can lead to wasted time and effort. Foster open lines of communication where team members feel comfortable seeking clarification. Promote concise and

clear communication to minimize back-and-forth exchanges.

8. **Procrastination**: Delaying tasks can create a cycle of stress and missed deadlines. Encourage a proactive mindset by breaking tasks into smaller, manageable pieces and setting deadlines to maintain momentum.

9. **Social media and Digital Distractions**: The lure of social media can be a significant time sink. Encourage your team to set boundaries around digital distractions and utilize tools that block these sites during work hours, ensuring focus on critical tasks.

10. **Overcommitment**: Taking on too many responsibilities can lead to burnout and decreased productivity. Teach your team the importance of understanding their limits and empower them to say no when necessary. This not only preserves individual capacity but also enhances overall team effectiveness.

11. **Lack of Focus**: Frequent task-switching can diminish overall productivity. Encourage practices that promote deep work, such as time-blocking or the Pomodoro Technique, to help team members concentrate on one task at a time.

12. **Failure to Reflect and Adjust**: Neglecting to review what is working and what isn't can perpetuate inefficiencies. Promote regular check-ins and reflection sessions where the team can assess their time management practices and make necessary adjustments.

By addressing these common time wasters, you empower your team to manage their time more effectively. As a servant leader, your commitment to fostering a culture of awareness and adaptability not only enhances productivity but also builds a supportive environment where everyone can thrive. Remember, effective time management is not just about doing more—it's about achieving meaningful results together.

KEY STRATEGIES FOR EFFECTIVE TIME MANAGEMENT FOR PRODUCTIVITY

1. **Get Enough Sleep**: Prioritize rest by adjusting your bedtime to ensure you are well-rested. A refreshed mind is more focused, creative, and productive. As a servant leader, modeling good sleep habits can encourage your team to value their own well-being, creating a culture where health is seen as integral to success.

2. **Set an Alarm**: Utilize alarms and reminders to keep track of departure times, deadlines, and important tasks. This simple tool can help mitigate stress and ensure that you stay on schedule, allowing you to be more present and engaged in your work. Consider using different tones for different types of reminders to create an auditory cue that enhances your focus.

3. **Plan Ahead**: Take time each evening to prepare for the next day. Organize tasks, select outfits, and gather necessary materials to streamline your morning routine. This proactive approach reduces chaos and sets a positive tone for the day ahead, giving you a sense of control that can improve overall morale.

4. **Write It Down**: Capture all appointments, deadlines, and important tasks in a reliable calendar or planner. Writing things down not only reinforces memory but also creates a visual roadmap to guide your day, helping you stay organized and focused. Incorporate a habit of journaling to reflect on your achievements and challenges, which can provide valuable insights over time.

5. **Stick to the Plan**: Resist the urge to squeeze in extra tasks at the last minute. Prioritize your commitments and leave space for transitions. Respecting your time— and that of others— builds a culture of accountability and efficiency. Create "buffer zones" in your schedule to accommodate unexpected events or important discussions.

6. **Arrive Early**: Aim to arrive at meetings or appointments 10 minutes early. This not only accounts for unforeseen delays but also provides a window to gather your thoughts, review materials, or engage in brief, meaningful conversations with colleagues. Use this time for reflection or to set intentions for the meeting.

7. **Track Your Time**: Regularly monitor how long specific tasks take. This practice allows you to identify patterns, make informed adjustments to your planning, and ultimately enhance your efficiency. Consider using time-tracking apps that provide insights into how your time is spent, helping you identify areas for improvement.

8. **Embrace Mindfulness**: Integrate mindfulness practices into your daily routine. Taking a few moments for deep breathing or meditation can center your thoughts, enhance focus, and reduce stress. As a servant leader, promoting mindfulness can foster a more serene and productive work environment.

9. **Establish Boundaries**: Clearly define your work hours and communicate these boundaries to your team. Encouraging everyone to respect work-life balance helps prevent burnout and fosters a culture of mutual respect. When team members see you uphold these boundaries, they're more likely to do the same.

10. **Utilize the Two-Minute Rule**: If a task takes less than two minutes to complete, do it immediately. This simple rule can significantly reduce your to-do list and prevent minor tasks from piling up. It also cultivates a sense of accomplishment, propelling you forward throughout the day.

11. **Reflect and Adjust**: At the end of each week, take time to reflect on what worked and what didn't. Assess your successes and setbacks, and adjust your strategies accordingly. This reflective practice not only improves your time management but also deepens your self-awareness and adaptability.

12. **Cultivate a Supportive Environment**: Encourage open communication within your team about time management challenges. Create a space where individuals feel comfortable discussing their workloads and seeking help when needed. A supportive culture amplifies collective productivity and morale.

By embracing these transformative strategies, servant leaders can shape a culture of effective time management that not only amplifies individual productivity but also fosters an environment of collaboration, support, and mutual respect. When every team member feels valued and empowered, time management evolves from a basic skill into a shared organizational ethos—a cornerstone of success.

As Stephen Covey profoundly stated, *"The key is in not spending time, but in investing it."* Leaders who model this mindset set a powerful precedent, demonstrating that true productivity stems from purposeful time investment, balance, and a commitment to well-being.

In doing so, you cultivate a workplace where success and fulfillment coexist—where individuals not only achieve their goals but also thrive as part of a unified and dynamic team.

Remember, time is the most precious currency we have. Use it intentionally to advance your purpose, create value, and inspire others to do the same. Invest in what matters most, and you'll pave the way for extraordinary personal and professional growth.

Mastering Time: Your Most Valuable Asset

Time is the one resource we can never replenish, making its management the ultimate skill for success. In our fast-paced world, effective time management is not just about getting more done—it's about aligning your efforts with your values and goals to create a life of purpose and fulfillment.

As Benjamin Franklin wisely said, *"You may delay, but time will not."* The way you choose to spend your time defines your legacy and determines the opportunities you create. Understanding and mastering this precious resource can transform your life, enabling you to lead with clarity, achieve with intention, and inspire those around you.

The following are ERW's 12-Point Essential Elements of Time Management—a comprehensive guide designed to help you harness the power of time, boost your productivity, and create lasting impact.

ERW's 12-Point Essential Elements of Time Management

1. Planning

"Give me six hours to chop down a tree, and I will spend the first four sharpening my ax." — Abraham Lincoln. Planning is the cornerstone of effective time management. Differentiate between urgent and important tasks, and set clear goals—short-term, midterm, and long-term. Each day, identify your top three tasks, prioritize them, and tackle them in order of significance.

2. Never Waste Time

Time wasted is life wasted. Ephesians 5:11 advises, *"Expose these things for the sham they are."* Alan Laken aptly states, *"Time = life; therefore, waste your time and waste your life. Master your time and master your life."*

3. Invest Your Time

Productive time investment leads to prosperity and fulfillment. As Michael Altshuler noted, *"The bad news is time flies, but the good news is, you are the pilot."* Your actions today define tomorrow's success.

4. Work Smarter, Not Harder

Time management is about efficiency, not exhaustion. Focus on critical tasks, breaking them into manageable steps. Being busy doesn't always mean being productive.

5. Delegate

Maximize productivity by empowering your team. Harry S. Truman said it best: *"It's amazing what you can accomplish if you do not care who gets the credit."* Effective delegation is essential to leadership.

6. Learn to Say No

Saying no preserves your focus and integrity. Tony Robbins reminds us, *"Saying 'no' is not an insult but a means to safeguard your time and purpose."*

7. Urgent vs. Important

Stephen R. Covey emphasized the need to prioritize importance over urgency. Deep work requires undivided focus, free from interruptions.

8. The Battle Plan

Tackle your day with a strategic approach. As Dwight D. Eisenhower said, *"In preparing for battle, I have always found that plans are useless, but planning is indispensable."*

9. Discipline and Deadlines

Discipline ensures progress. Amit Kalantari reminds us, *"We must all suffer one of two things: the pain of discipline or the pain of regret."* Setting and meeting deadlines fuels growth.

10. Avoid Multitasking

Multitasking reduces quality and increases errors. Focus on one task at a time to maintain excellence and efficiency.

11. Wasted Talent

Talent without effort is squandered. Tim Notke said, *"Hard work beats talent when talent doesn't work hard."* Effective time management ensures talent shines through.

12. Use Technology Wisely

Let technology be your tool, not a distraction. Avoid social media and email interruptions, and use productivity tools to enhance, not hinder, your focus.

CONCLUSION

Mastering time management is a lifelong journey requiring strategy, reflection, and discipline. It is not just about achieving personal growth but empowering those around you to reach their potential. As Mahatma Gandhi once said, *"The best way to find yourself is to lose yourself in the service of others."*

By embracing these principles, you turn time into an ally rather than an adversary. Remember, time is not merely a resource; it is the canvas on which you paint your legacy. Use it wisely, and you will shape not only your destiny but also the world around you.

THE POWER OF INTUITION

INTRODUCTION

Intuition: The Superpower of Effective Decision-Making

Intuition is a form of intelligence that transcends rationality, reasoning, and data analysis, making it an indispensable asset in impactful decision-making. In an era where leaders across business, government, and families face increasingly complex challenges, the ability to make sound decisions is paramount. This chapter is designed to refine the intuition of top executives, entrepreneurs, and global leaders, empowering them to harness this divine gift to achieve extraordinary results.

As an entrepreneur and leader, decision-making is both the most challenging and fulfilling aspect of my journey. Over two decades of leadership roles have taught me that success hinges on the ability to make pivotal decisions. My secret weapon? Intuition. Oprah Winfrey perfectly encapsulates its power: *"Trust your instincts. Intuition doesn't lie."*

Decisions are catalysts for action and outcomes—whether triumphs or setbacks. Even the absence of a decision is a decision, often leaving progress to chance and inviting uncertainty or failure. As a servant leader, your role is to act decisively, often under pressure. It is in these moments that intuition becomes your superpower, enabling you to respond swiftly and effectively.

Every decision carries the potential to drive unparalleled success, lead to stagnation, or risk failure.

This chapter will guide you in understanding, cultivating, and applying intuition to make decisions that create groundbreaking outcomes and lasting impact. By mastering the balance between intuition and data-driven insights, you'll unlock the ability to make choices that define your legacy.

Intuition – The Servant Leader's Compass

Intuition, in the context of servant leadership, is the innate ability to instinctively grasp and respond to situations without relying solely on data or analysis. It represents a deep, subconscious awareness that blends past experiences, emotional intelligence, and a keen understanding of people and environments.

For servant leaders, intuition is a guiding compass, enabling decisions that prioritize the growth and well-being of those they lead. It helps uncover hidden issues, identify opportunities, and navigate the intricacies of human interaction. By trusting their intuition, servant leaders cultivate authenticity and openness, inspiring their teams to collaborate and align with shared objectives.

Intuition is far more than a fleeting feeling or a random guess—it is a refined awareness that unites insight, empathy, and foresight. This indispensable quality empowers leaders to make impactful decisions and foster a culture where individuals thrive and organizations flourish.

THE DIFFERENT LEVELS AND CHARACTERISTICS OF DECISION-MAKING – A SERVANT LEADER'S PERSPECTIVE

Decision-making is the cornerstone of effective leadership, shaping outcomes that range from minor successes to transformative breakthroughs. For servant leaders, every decision reflects their commitment to empowering others and driving meaningful change. By understanding the different levels of decisions—bad, OK, good, great, and GOAT—you gain clarity on how to harness intuition, balance impulsivity, and cultivate foresight. This segment offers insights to help you elevate your decision-making, ensuring your choices leave a lasting, positive impact.

1. Bad Decisions: Void of Intuition and Foresight

Bad decisions often arise from poor judgment, lack of insight, or ignoring intuition. These choices can lead to catastrophic consequences, such as Adolf Hitler's decision to invade Poland in 1939, sparking World War II. Bad decisions undermine trust, cause irreparable harm, and often stem from flawed reasoning or insufficient information.

2. OK Decisions: Overriding Intuition

OK decisions are typically safe but uninspired. These occur when leaders suppress their instincts to follow trends or conventional thinking. While such decisions may lead to moderate success, they often lack the transformative power of intuition-driven choices.

3. Good Decisions: Noticeable and Beneficial

Good decisions blend intuition with logical analysis to create meaningful outcomes. For example, an entrepreneur trusting their instincts to pivot strategies based on customer feedback can achieve substantial success. These decisions enhance effectiveness and demonstrate the power of balanced judgment.

4. Great Decisions: Significant Impact

Great decisions take calculated risks and involve innovative thinking, leading to groundbreaking changes. For example, leaders like Jeff Bezos have transformed industries by combining intuition with data to identify untapped opportunities, achieving massive growth and expansion.

5. GOAT (Greatest of All Time) Decisions: History-Making Choices

GOAT-level decisions reshape history and establish new paradigms. Visionary leaders like Thomas Edison, who pursued the practical incandescent light bulb despite skepticism, demonstrate how perseverance and intuition can revolutionize society.

IMPULSIVE DECISIONS – SERVANT LEADER'S ADVICE

Impulsive decisions can sometimes yield remarkable outcomes when aligned with core values and guided by a servant leader's intuition. However, these should be exercised responsibly.

Key Principles for Responsible Impulsivity:

1. **Align with Core Values:** Ensure impulsive actions align with your mission to maintain trust and integrity.
2. **Assess the Impact:** Evaluate potential consequences before acting to balance urgency with responsibility.

3. **Foster Openness:** Cultivate a collaborative environment where team input strengthens decision-making.
4. **Learn from Outcomes:** Reflect on results to refine intuition and improve future decisions.
5. **Balance Intuition with Insight:** Combine instinct with data for holistic, impactful choices.

By understanding the spectrum of decision-making—from bad to GOAT-level—and responsibly leveraging intuition, servant leaders can inspire their teams, create transformative change, and lead with purpose. As you navigate these levels, remember that every decision shapes not only outcomes but also your legacy as a leader.

ANALYTICAL MIND VS. INTUITIVE MIND: KEY DISTINCTIONS

In the complex world of decision-making, two cognitive approaches stand out: the analytical mind and the intuitive mind. Both offer distinct strengths, and understanding their differences can help leaders navigate challenges more effectively. The analytical mind is grounded in logic, data, and structure, while the intuitive mind relies on gut feelings, pattern recognition, and quick insights. This segment explores the key distinctions between these two approaches, highlighting how each contributes to effective decision-making and how leaders can harness both to achieve remarkable outcomes.

1. Analytical Mind:

- **Logical and Rational:** The analytical mind thrives on structured frameworks, emphasizing logical reasoning and systematic problem-solving. It is crucial in fields like finance and engineering, where precision and accuracy are paramount. Research by Thagard (2006) underscores the importance of logical reasoning for scientific inquiry and effective decision-making.

- **Relies on Facts, Evidence, and Reasoning:** Analytical decision-making is based on quantifiable data and thorough research. Ghosh and Khedkar (2016) highlight that evidence-based decision-making significantly enhances organizational performance, especially in high-stakes scenarios.
- **Breaks Down Problems into Smaller Parts:** This cognitive style excels in deconstructing complex issues into manageable components, allowing leaders to identify root causes and devise effective solutions (Paul & Elder, 2006).
- **Prefers Structure and Order:** Analytical thinkers thrive in organized environments, where structured settings reduce ambiguity and enable clearer pathways to conclusions (Schmitt et al., 2015).
- **Associated with the Left Hemisphere of the Brain:** The left hemisphere plays a key role in analytical thought processes, particularly in tasks requiring logic and detailed analysis (Kosslyn & Miller, 2002).

2. Intuitive Mind:

- **Relies on Gut Feelings, Hunches, or Instincts:** The intuitive mind often guides decision-making through instinctual responses, enabling quick and effective choices. Kahneman (2011) notes that intuition can be crucial in environments where time constraints limit detailed analysis.
- **Processes Information Quickly, Often Without Conscious Reasoning:** Intuition synthesizes vast

amounts of information rapidly, bypassing detailed deliberation. Gladwell (2005) emphasizes the power of rapid cognition, suggesting that instinctual judgments can sometimes be more accurate than deliberate thought.

- **Sees the Bigger Picture and Makes Connections:** Intuitive thinkers excel at recognizing patterns and understanding complex systems. Simon (1996) suggests that intuition allows for a holistic grasp of situations, enabling leaders to navigate uncertainty with confidence.
- **Thrives in Ambiguity:** Intuitive minds are especially adept at operating in uncertain environments, where quick decisions are necessary. Gigerenzer (2007) suggests that intuition often surpasses analytical thought in such scenarios.
- **Associated with the Right Hemisphere of the Brain:** The right hemisphere, linked to creativity and emotional intelligence, plays a critical role in intuitive decision-making. Laureys et al. (2010) found that right-brain functions support intuition by allowing individuals to draw on personal experiences and emotional insights.

The Balance of Both Minds

Albert Einstein once called intuition a "precious gift," illustrating its value alongside rational thought. While analytical thinking is essential for dissecting challenges and making informed decisions, intuition provides invaluable insights that can lead to groundbreaking solutions. By integrating both cognitive styles, leaders can enhance their decision-making abilities, fostering innovation, resilience, and better outcomes in today's rapidly changing world. Balancing analytical rigor with intuitive insight enables leaders to navigate complexities effectively and inspire their teams to achieve remarkable success.

THE ROLE OF INTUITION IN DECISION-MAKING: THE SERVANT LEADER'S GUIDE

"Data is a tool for enhancing intuition." — Hilary Mason

In a world defined by rapid change and uncertainty, the ability to make quick, yet informed decisions are more vital than ever. As a servant leader, the power of balancing intuition with data can transform your decision-making process, helping you act swiftly while remaining grounded in insight. This blend of gut feeling and empirical evidence not only enhances the quality of your choices but also fuels your ability to inspire and guide your team through any challenge.

1. Finding the Balance

Intuition as a Compass: Intuition is your inner guide, drawing from experience and subconscious knowledge to navigate the unknown. As Kahneman (2011) suggests, it's your secret weapon when time is critical, enabling decisions with confidence and speed.

Data as Your Foundation: While intuition offers direction, data gives you the grounding to make informed choices. Provost and Fawcett (2013) highlight how data-driven insights ensure your hunches are solid, preventing costly missteps.

2. Harnessing the Power of Both

Critical Thinking & Empathy: To make better decisions, you must blend intuition with critical thinking. By analyzing data and understanding the human aspect through empathy, you'll refine your instincts into well-rounded strategies. Goleman (2006) reminds us that emotional intelligence builds deep connections that elevate leadership.

Foresight & Vision: When combined with data, intuition enhances your ability to predict future trends, giving you an edge in identifying opportunities and mitigating risks. This synergy empowers you to lead with foresight and confidence.

3. Navigating Complexity

Speed vs. Accuracy: Effective leadership demands both rapid decision-making and informed choices. Striking the right balance between these elements enables you to act decisively without compromising quality, as Eisenhardt and Zbaracki (1992) affirm.

Adaptability in Uncertainty: Trusting your intuition, while supporting it with data, allows you to pivot quickly in the face of uncertainty. McKinsey & Company (2020) highlights that leaders who cultivate adaptability will thrive in a volatile business landscape.

4. Achieving Exceptional Results

Empowerment through Collaboration: When you create an environment where team input is valued, intuition and data become even more powerful. Edmondson (2012) underscores that fostering psychological safety encourages deeper collaboration and innovative decision-making.

Continuous Learning: Every decision offers an opportunity for growth. By reflecting on outcomes and seeking feedback, you refine both your intuitive abilities and data analysis, ensuring future decisions align with your broader organizational goals.

In Conclusion: By mastering the integration of intuition and data, you unlock a potent leadership tool that drives confidence, fosters adaptability, and delivers extraordinary results. As you embrace both your gut and your data, remember that every decision is a step toward success—for both you and your team.

DIFFERENTIATING INSTINCT FROM INTUITION: A SCIENTIFIC PERSPECTIVE

Understanding the subtle differences between instinct and intuition is essential for leaders seeking to make sound decisions in complex environments. Though both processes influence decision-making, they stem from different cognitive mechanisms and serve distinct purposes.

1. Instinct: The Survival Mechanism

Definition: Instincts are innate, automatic reactions hardwired into our biology. These responses are triggered by immediate threats or stimuli, typically focused on survival.

Functionality: Instincts operate reflexively at a subconscious level. For example, the fight-or-flight response kicks in when danger is perceived, prompting rapid, unconscious action to ensure survival. This mechanism, honed over millennia of evolutionary pressure, is critical in moments requiring quick, life-preserving decisions (Buss, 2009).

Characteristics: Instincts are binary and immediate, driven by physiological cues and ingrained behavior patterns. They lack the influence of personal experience or long-term considerations, focusing solely on immediate safety and survival.

2. Intuition: The Forward-Thinking Compass

Definition: Intuition, by contrast, is a more complex cognitive process that integrates past experiences, knowledge, and subconscious insights to guide decisions.

Functionality: Intuition is often described as a "gut feeling" that emerges after subconscious analysis of a variety of factors. It enables individuals to make informed judgments and envision potential outcomes based on a broader context (Dane & Pratt, 2007).

Characteristics: Intuitive insights are typically marked by a sense of familiarity, alignment with personal values, and a holistic view of a situation. Unlike instinct, intuition involves a deeper synthesis of cognitive and emotional factors, reflecting a long-term and goal-oriented perspective.

3. Scientific Distinctions Between Instinct and Intuition

Cognitive Processing: Instinct operates mainly through the limbic system, which governs emotional responses, whereas intuition engages higher-order cognitive functions within the prefrontal cortex (Damasio, 1994). This distinction underscores the complexity of intuition, which involves conscious thought and processing, as opposed to the reflexive, primal nature of instinct.

Temporal Aspect: Instinct is immediate and reactive, responding to present threats, while intuition often carries an anticipatory element. Intuition allows individuals to synthesize past experiences and predict future outcomes, a process absent from instinctual reactions (Kahneman, 2011).

4. Practical Implications for Leadership

Application in Decision-Making: Effective leaders must understand when to rely on instinct for swift decisions in crises and when to engage their intuition for more strategic, long-term planning. Recognizing the appropriate context for each can amplify a leader's decision-making effectiveness, enabling them to act decisively when necessary and thoughtfully when it counts.

Fostering Intuitive Skills: Developing intuitive capabilities requires deliberate reflection and continuous learning. Leaders can enhance their intuition by reviewing past decisions, seeking feedback, and actively cultivating emotional intelligence. A well-honed intuition allows leaders to make more informed, values-driven choices that benefit their teams, foster trust, and drive organizational success.

In summary, while instinct serves as an immediate, survival-driven response, intuition acts as a forward-thinking guide, synthesizing past experiences with future possibilities. By understanding these distinctions, leaders can leverage both instinct and intuition to navigate challenges effectively. Developing and balancing these skills not only helps leaders make more nuanced decisions but also fosters resilience and adaptability, ensuring sustained success for both themselves and their organizations.

THE PHYSIOLOGY OF INTUITION

Intuition is not just a vague or mystical phenomenon; it is deeply embedded in the physiology of the brain and body. The way we make intuitive decisions is shaped by complex neurochemical processes that influence how we recognize patterns, assess risks, and anticipate outcomes.

Neurotransmitters and Their Impact

1. **Dopamine**: Often called the "feel-good" neurotransmitter, dopamine plays a pivotal role in motivation, pleasure, and reward. It enhances our ability to recognize patterns, anticipate outcomes, and make decisions based on past experiences. When we feel excitement or motivation about a decision, dopamine is actively shaping our intuitive responses. Increased

dopamine levels can also boost creativity and openness to new ideas, promoting more fluid and adaptive decision-making.

2. **Serotonin**: Known for regulating mood and fostering feelings of well-being, serotonin is crucial for clarity and focus in decision-making. Optimal serotonin levels help calm the nervous system, reducing anxiety and allowing individuals to trust their instincts. This stability enhances intuitive thinking, enabling more confident and well-balanced decisions.
3. **The Interaction of Emotions and Intuition**: Emotional states—regulated by neurotransmitters—have a profound influence on intuition. Positive emotions, facilitated by balanced dopamine and serotonin levels, can heighten intuitive insights, while negative emotions, often triggered by stress, can cloud judgment. When under pressure, the brain may default to a fight-or-flight response, potentially sidelining the nuanced and reflective thought processes that intuition relies on.
4. **The Role of the Limbic System**: The limbic system, including the amygdala and hippocampus, is essential for processing emotions and memories that inform intuitive decisions. The amygdala evaluates the emotional significance of stimuli, while the hippocampus retrieves past experiences, helping us draw on previous knowledge in new situations. Together, these structures lay the groundwork for intuition, enabling us to respond based on past emotional cues and learned experiences.

In summary, intuition is the result of a sophisticated interplay between neurochemical processes, emotions, and cognitive functions. Understanding the physiological underpinnings of intuition allows leaders to harness its power for more informed and impactful decision-making. By cultivating emotional well-being and fostering environments that stimulate motivation, leaders can enhance their intuitive abilities, driving better decisions both personally and professionally.

Does Intuition Vary by Gender? The Servant Leader's Perspective

Research suggests that intuition is a universally valuable tool for decision-making, regardless of gender. Both men and women recognize its importance in leadership, although subtle differences in how intuition is framed can emerge. Studies have shown that women may be more likely to use terms like "gut feel" rather than "intuition," possibly to avoid gender biases and stereotypes that can arise in professional environments (Mason, 2016). While this linguistic distinction exists, it does not change the essential role intuition plays for all leaders.

From a servant leader's perspective, it is crucial to acknowledge and celebrate the intuitive abilities inherent in every individual. Intuition allows leaders to navigate complexity with empathy, understanding, and insight, fostering inclusive environments where diverse perspectives are embraced. Intuitive insights bridge the gap between data-driven decision-making and emotional intelligence, helping leaders connect with their teams and cultivate meaningful relationships.

Ultimately, intuition is not confined by gender—it is a shared human experience that enhances the leadership journey. By embracing intuition, leaders can make more impactful, values-driven decisions, creating environments where everyone feels heard, understood, and empowered.

BALANCING INTUITION AND DATA-DRIVEN DECISIONS – THE SERVANT LEADER'S GUIDE

Albert Einstein, the Nobel Prize-winning physicist, once acknowledged the pivotal role intuition plays in guiding discoveries, particularly in uncharted territories. In today's fast-paced, data-driven world, the challenge for effective leaders is finding a harmonious balance between intuition and data-informed decisions.

Cultivating Intuition Alongside Data Analysis

Leaders who develop both intuitive insight and strong data analysis skills can elevate their decision-making. This combined approach allows them to use data to validate and refine intuitive judgments while allowing intuition to guide them through situations where data alone may not provide clarity. Intuition becomes the compass, while data provides the map.

The Servant Leader's Perspective

From a servant leader's point of view, the interplay of intuition and data is crucial for creating a culture of trust and collaboration. By encouraging team members to contribute their intuitive insights, leaders foster an environment where diverse perspectives are valued. This inclusivity empowers individuals to feel ownership in the decision-making process, strengthening their connection to the organization's mission and goals.

In my leadership journey, I have found that when data is integrated with intuition, decisions are made with greater confidence and accuracy. This balanced approach helps leaders navigate uncertainties, adapt to changing circumstances, and drive positive organizational outcomes.

Achieving Greater Outcomes

When leaders embrace both intuition and data, they unlock greater potential for innovation and growth. This synergy transforms challenges into opportunities, allowing organizations to thrive. By leveraging both data and intuitive wisdom, leaders inspire creativity, resilience, and adaptability, ensuring long-term success in the face of constant change.

The Payoff of Intuitive Leadership – A Servant Leadership Perspective

Intuition, often misunderstood or dismissed as mere happenstance, is actually a profound cognitive phenomenon deeply rooted in neuroscience. It's not random; instead, it draws from a wealth of past experiences, emotional responses, and subconscious knowledge. This internal compass, shaped by emotional tagging, guides leaders through complex decisions and offers insights that transcend data alone.

Success Stories and Benefits of Intuition-Driven Leadership

As Oprah Winfrey aptly stated, "I've trusted the still small voice of intuition my entire life. And, the only time I've made mistakes is when I didn't listen." This captures the heart of intuition as a vital tool for leadership. Many of the world's most successful leaders have credited their intuition with guiding them through crucial moments in their careers.

Take Howard Schultz, for example. His intuitive understanding of the human desire for connection and community led him to create Starbucks' experience-centric coffee culture. Recognizing that people craved more than just a caffeine fix, he crafted a space where customers could feel a sense of belonging. This vision transformed Starbucks into a global brand that resonated deeply with consumers.

Similarly, Satya Nadella's intuitive grasp of empathy and a growth mindset revitalized Microsoft, shifting its culture to one of innovation, collaboration, and inclusivity. Nadella's ability to connect with his teams on a human level enabled him to drive Microsoft's transformation, making it a more agile and forward-thinking company.

The benefits of intuition-driven leadership extend beyond individual success stories. Organizations led by intuitive leaders experience enhanced creativity, improved problem-solving capabilities, and greater employee engagement. When leaders embrace intuition alongside analytical thinking, they create a space where diverse perspectives thrive, leading to more comprehensive and resilient decision-making.

How Intuition Enhances Leadership Effectiveness and Vision

Jeff Bezos once said, "When you can make a decision with analysis, you should do so, but it turns out in life that your most important decisions are always made with instinct, intuition, taste, heart." In an ever-evolving leadership landscape, intuition proves to be an essential ally. While data-driven decisions provide a solid foundation, it is intuition that refines and elevates those decisions, allowing leaders to navigate uncertainty with clarity.

Intuition empowers leaders to align their decisions with core values and ethical principles. It enables them to make choices that not only drive organizational success but also uphold the integrity and mission of the team or company. When intuitive leadership is coupled with a deep understanding of one's purpose and values, it fosters a culture of trust, adaptability, and resilience.

Cultivating intuition as a core aspect of leadership is a powerful strategy that can significantly enhance decision-making. It transforms leaders into visionaries who can navigate complexity with confidence, adaptability, and insight. As servant leaders, embracing intuition enables us to empower our teams, create meaningful connections, and achieve long-term success—both individually and as organizations.

THE ROLE OF INTUITION IN MODERN LEADERSHIP

In today's rapidly evolving and complex world, intuition plays a pivotal role in effective leadership. While data and analysis are essential, intuitive insights empower leaders to make more adaptive, empathetic, and innovative decisions.

1. Navigating Complexity:

Intuition allows leaders to quickly synthesize vast amounts of information, enabling them to identify patterns and insights that may not be immediately obvious through data alone. This is particularly valuable in high-pressure environments where timely decisions are critical. Intuition aids in making swift judgments even when there is uncertainty or incomplete information, guiding leaders through ambiguity.

2. Fostering Authenticity:

Leaders who trust their intuition are often more authentic in their decision-making. They align their choices with personal values, which in turn inspires trust and loyalty from their teams. This authenticity helps build an environment of openness and collaboration, where team members feel heard and respected, contributing to a positive organizational culture.

3. Encouraging Innovation:

Intuitive thinking fosters creativity and encourages leaders to explore new avenues and ideas that may not be evident through traditional, data-driven methods. Leaders who tap into their instincts can identify opportunities for innovation and create novel solutions, often ahead of competitors. This openness to new ideas becomes a driving force for maintaining a competitive edge in dynamic markets.

4. Enhancing Emotional Intelligence:

Intuition is closely tied to emotional intelligence, which enables leaders to understand and respond to the emotional dynamics of their teams. Leaders with high emotional intelligence can read situations accurately, gauge the emotions of others, and adapt their approach accordingly. This ability strengthens relationships, enhances communication, and plays a key role in conflict resolution.

5. Empowering Decision-Making:

By combining intuition with analytical thinking, leaders can create a well-rounded decision-making framework. While analysis provides a rational basis for decisions, intuition ensures that those decisions resonate emotionally with the team. This holistic approach leads to more impactful and sustainable outcomes, as it balances both the logical and emotional aspects of leadership.

Case Example: Howard Schultz and Starbucks

Howard Schultz's transformation of Starbucks serves as a prime example of how intuition can drive visionary leadership. Schultz trusted his instincts about the evolving coffee culture and consumer desire for more than just a beverage. He saw the potential for Starbucks to become a community-focused brand, a "third place" between home and work, where customers could gather, relax, and connect. His intuition about the customer experience and the atmosphere of Starbucks revolutionized the coffee industry and helped build a brand that millions of people globally connect with emotionally.

Incorporating intuition into leadership allows for more dynamic, empathetic, and innovative decision-making. By balancing analytical rigor with intuitive insights, leaders are better equipped to navigate the complexities of the modern business landscape. This fusion not only drives organizational success but also fosters stronger, more authentic relationships between leaders and their teams. Intuitive leadership cultivates an environment where collaboration, creativity, and trust flourish, paving the way for long-term growth and success.

GROUNDBREAKING OUTCOMES OF INTUITIVE DECISION-MAKING: CASE STUDIES SHOWCASING REMARKABLE RESULTS

Intuitive decision-making has often been a catalyst for transformative breakthroughs in business. Leaders who rely on their instincts, coupled with a deep understanding of their industries and a willingness to take risks, have frequently achieved groundbreaking success. Here are some prominent examples:

1. Airbnb: A $35 Billion Enterprise Built on Intuition

Airbnb's rise is a powerful testament to the value of intuition in entrepreneurship. Founders Brian Chesky and Joe Gebbia tapped into an unaddressed market need for affordable, short-term lodging by trusting their instincts. Despite facing skepticism about the viability of the model, their intuition about the potential of home-sharing led to the creation of a global community-oriented platform. This decision revolutionized the hospitality industry and propelled Airbnb into a $35 billion business.

2. Tesla and Elon Musk: Disrupting the Electric Vehicle Market

Elon Musk's leadership at Tesla has been marked by bold, intuitive decisions that have reshaped entire industries. Musk's decision to enter the electric vehicle market was driven by a strong, gut feeling about the future of sustainable energy. He trusted his instincts despite the lack of early data supporting electric vehicle adoption. As a result, Tesla has become a leader in innovation, pushing the boundaries of technology and sustainability, and achieving a market valuation of over $800 billion.

3. Netflix and Reed Hastings: Transitioning from DVDs to Streaming

Reed Hastings, co-founder of Netflix, demonstrated the power of intuition when he decided to pivot from DVD rentals to streaming services in the early 2000s. He sensed the changing dynamics of consumer behavior and saw the future of entertainment shifting towards digital streaming. This decision, initially met with skepticism, propelled Netflix into the global entertainment powerhouse it is today, with over 200 million subscribers worldwide.

4. Google and Sergey Brin: Transforming Search with PageRank

Sergey Brin's decision to develop Google's search algorithm based on the principles of link analysis was an intuitive leap that reshaped the internet. Brin's belief in the importance of how websites link to one another led to the creation of PageRank, which ultimately became the foundation for Google's search engine. This innovation transformed Google into the world's leading search engine and fundamentally changed how information is accessed and consumed online.

5. **Walt Disney Company:**

Walt Disney's intuitive sense of storytelling and entertainment revolutionized the animation industry. His decision to create full-length animated features, starting with "Snow White and the Seven Dwarfs," was initially met with skepticism. However, Disney's intuition about audiences' desires for engaging narratives paved the way for a new era in film and entertainment, establishing Disney as a cultural icon.

6. Spotify:

Daniel Ek, co-founder of Spotify, utilized his intuition when he envisioned a streaming platform that would combat music piracy while providing a better user experience. His understanding of consumer behavior and the music industry led to innovations in music consumption, such as personalized playlists and algorithm-driven recommendations, transforming how people access music.

7. LEGO:

After facing declining sales, LEGO's leadership relied on intuition to pivot the company back to its core strengths. By engaging with fans and leveraging their feedback, they launched the LEGO Ideas platform, allowing fans to submit and vote on new product designs. This intuitive move not only revitalized the brand but also fostered a strong community around LEGO products.

These case studies illustrate how intuition plays a crucial role in driving innovation across various industries. By trusting their instincts and embracing creative risks, these leaders were able to push boundaries and achieve remarkable success. Integrating intuition with strategic planning can empower servant leaders to cultivate an environment ripe for innovation, ensuring that their organizations remain adaptable and competitive in a rapidly changing world.

The Power of Intuition in Leadership

A 2018 KPMG study found that 67% of CEOs rely on their intuition, even when it contradicts data. This instinctive judgment allows leaders to navigate ambiguity and seize opportunities that data alone may not reveal. Steve Jobs famously said, "Intuition is a very powerful thing, more powerful than intellect." His leadership at Apple was shaped by this belief, making decisions based on gut feelings that led to groundbreaking products like the iPhone and iPad.

These case studies highlight the profound impact that intuitive decision-making can have on organizational success. By trusting their instincts, leaders can make bold choices that drive innovation and lead to remarkable outcomes. In today's fast-paced business world, intuition enables leaders to navigate uncertainty, uncover hidden opportunities, and steer their organizations toward unprecedented growth.

THE CRITICAL ROLE OF INTUITION IN FOSTERING INNOVATION – THE SERVANT LEADER'S APPROACH AND GUIDE

In the ever-evolving business world, innovation often arises from the ability to see beyond the conventional. While data provides valuable insights, true creativity stems from intuitive thinking that allows leaders to envision possibilities that others may overlook. Servant leaders, who prioritize the well-being and growth of their teams, have a unique opportunity to cultivate environments that harness the power of intuition to drive innovation.

The Role of Intuition in Innovation

Intuition allows leaders to make leaps in thinking, uncovering new solutions and ideas that may not be immediately evident through data or analysis. It is this ability to think creatively and embrace ambiguity that sparks transformative breakthroughs. For servant leaders, fostering an atmosphere where intuition can flourish not only enhances innovation but also empowers teams to contribute their best ideas.

KEY STRATEGIES FOR LEVERAGING INTUITION TO FOSTER INNOVATION

1. **Encourage Open Dialogue:**
    - Create spaces where team members feel safe to express their ideas and instincts. Open dialogue allows diverse perspectives to emerge, leading to the birth of innovative ideas that might otherwise remain untapped.
2. **Embrace Ambiguity:**
    - Understand that not all decisions can be supported by concrete data. Embrace uncertainty and give room for intuitive insights to guide decision-making. This flexibility can often lead to unexpected creative breakthroughs.
3. **Integrate Intuition with Data:**
    - While intuition is invaluable, it should be complemented by data analysis. Combining both approaches ensures a balanced decision-making process that is both informed and innovative, making it easier to navigate complex situations.

4. **Promote Continuous Learning:**
    - Encourage your team to explore various fields, ideas, and experiences. The broader their knowledge base, the more intuitive insights they can draw upon when faced with challenges. Lifelong learning fosters a rich environment for creativity and intuitive thinking.
5. **Celebrate Failures as Learning Opportunities:**
    - Cultivate a mindset that views failure as a learning experience. This approach frees team members from the fear of making mistakes and encourages them to take intuitive risks, which is often where innovation occurs.
6. **Lead by Example:**
    - Demonstrate your own intuitive decision-making processes. Share your experiences and insights from following your instincts, reinforcing the value of intuition in driving innovation. As a servant leader, modeling this behavior helps normalize intuition within the team.
7. **Create a Visionary Culture:**
    - Inspire your team with a clear, forward-thinking vision that encourages innovative thinking. A shared purpose aligns intuitive insights with organizational goals, fostering a collaborative and inventive culture that drives progress.

In today's fast-paced and complex world, the interplay between intuition and innovation is essential. Servant leaders who embrace intuition as a critical component of the creative process can empower their teams to think outside the box, overcome challenges, and make groundbreaking advancements. By fostering a culture that encourages intuitive decision-making and creative thinking, leaders can unlock new opportunities, drive sustained growth, and create a competitive advantage that propels organizations toward success.

In embracing intuition, servant leaders have the power to shape a future where creativity and innovation are at the heart of every decision, and every team member is empowered to contribute to a brighter outcome.

CULTIVATING INTUITION: A SERVANT LEADER'S GUIDE TO CLARITY

As a servant leader, fostering intuition within yourself and your team can lead to clearer, more confident decision-making. Here are practical steps for developing and trusting your intuition, supported by research and proven strategies:

1. **Prayer and Meditation:** Engaging in spiritual practices like prayer and meditation fosters a deeper connection with your inner self, improving emotional regulation and self-awareness. Research (Keng et al., 2011) shows that mindfulness meditation enhances these abilities, leading to clearer decision-making. Leaders who engage in meditation often experience increased clarity in their thought processes.
2. **Mindfulness:** Incorporating mindfulness techniques into daily routines heightens awareness of your thoughts, emotions, and reactions. A study by Zeidan et al. (2010) found that mindfulness meditation improves cognitive flexibility, enabling leaders to make more effective decisions, particularly in complex or ambiguous situations.
3. **Reflective Journaling:** Regular journaling encourages leaders to reflect on past decisions and the intuitive processes behind them. Research by Pennebaker (1997)

suggests that expressive writing enhances cognitive processing and emotional clarity, helping individuals understand and trust their intuitive insights more fully.

4. **Engaging in Nature:** Spending time in natural settings can significantly enhance your intuitive thinking. Kaplan and Kaplan (1989) suggest that exposure to nature fosters restorative experiences that improve focus and creativity, leading to clearer, more insightful decision-making.
5. **Seeking Diverse Perspectives:** Engaging with individuals from diverse backgrounds broadens your perspective and enhances intuitive thinking. Research by Page (2007) indicates that diversity of thought leads to better problem-solving, innovation, and more informed decisions, enriching your intuitive judgment.
6. **Practice Decision-Making:** Regularly practice decision-making in situations where intuition plays a key role. A study by Sadler-Smith and Badham (2018) emphasizes that repeated practice in intuitive decision-making boosts both accuracy and confidence in one's judgments, helping leaders make decisions with greater assurance.
7. **Foster a Safe Environment for Intuition:** Create a culture within your team where members feel safe to express their intuitive insights without fear of judgment. A supportive environment encourages open dialogue, allowing collective intuitive capacities to thrive (Edmondson, 1999). When team members feel valued for their intuitive contributions, the organization as a whole can benefit from enhanced creativity and problem-solving.

CASE STUDIES IN INTUITIVE LEADERSHIP

1. Richard Branson

The founder of the Virgin Group, Richard Branson, has long been an advocate for trusting intuition in business decisions. Branson is known for saying, "I rely far more on gut instinct than researching huge amounts of statistics." His success across diverse ventures, from airlines to music to space travel, highlights the power of intuitive leadership. Branson's approach reflects an ability to take bold risks based on instinct, often entering markets that others might deem too risky or uncertain. This intuition-driven mindset has been a key factor in Virgin's ability to disrupt multiple industries and carve out a distinct brand identity.

2. Steve Jobs

Steve Jobs, the late co-founder of Apple Inc., is another iconic example of intuitive leadership. Jobs famously stated, "Have the courage to follow your heart and intuition." His visionary approach to product development, from the iPhone to the iPad, was driven by intuition as much as data. Jobs believed that truly revolutionary products were not always the result of market research but rather came from trusting one's instincts about what consumers would want before they even knew it themselves. His leadership exemplifies how intuition can guide transformative innovation, even in highly competitive and rapidly evolving industries.

Cultivating Intuition in Servant Leadership

Cultivating intuition is essential for servant leaders who wish to make impactful decisions and drive innovation. By integrating practices like meditation, mindfulness, and reflective journaling, leaders can strengthen their intuitive capabilities, allowing them to make more confident and visionary decisions.

The success stories of **Richard Branson** and **Steve Jobs** serve as powerful reminders that trusting one's intuition can lead to extraordinary outcomes. Embracing intuition alongside analytical thinking empowers leaders to navigate complexities with clarity and conviction, ensuring that they not only lead with purpose but also inspire creativity and innovation within their organizations.

The Role of Intuition in Coaching and Athletic Performance

In sports, intuition is a critical tool that shapes performance and strategy. Known as "Basketball IQ" or "Game Sense," intuition enables athletes to make split-second decisions that can determine the outcome of a game. **LeBron James** exemplifies this, with his ability to read the game and anticipate plays, which enhances his decision-making under pressure. His basketball IQ integrates both experience and instinct, often leading to successful outcomes, such as executing the right pass or making a crucial drive to the basket.

Scientific research supports the role of intuition in sports. **Ericsson et al. (1993)** demonstrate that expert performers, like LeBron, develop a heightened ability to process complex patterns intuitively through years of practice and experience. This allows athletes to make decisions faster than they could through conscious reasoning alone. **Kramer et al. (2006)** found that athletes who integrate intuition with analytical insights perform better, as it combines the speed of intuitive decisions with the precision of data-driven analysis.

While data analytics have transformed sports, providing insights into performance metrics, intuition remains key. Research by **Raab and Johnson (2007)** highlights that coaches who blend intuitive judgment with statistical analysis gain a competitive edge, as intuition captures the nuanced, instinctive plays that data cannot fully account for. Thus, the synergy between intuition and data analytics is essential for peak performance, allowing athletes to make both informed and instinctual decisions.

By fostering an environment where athletes trust their intuition while leveraging data, coaches can optimize performance. This approach helps players transcend statistical limitations, enabling them to capitalize on the moments that truly matter. Intuition, supported by scientific findings, is indispensable in coaching and athletic performance.

Case Study: The Success of the Golden State Warriors

Under head coach **Steve Kerr**, the Golden State Warriors embody the effective blend of **intuition** and **data analytics**. Kerr places significant emphasis on fostering player intuition during games, encouraging players to trust their instincts and make creative decisions in real-time. This approach enables the team to adapt to evolving game situations and enhances overall performance. The Warriors' success lies in their ability to balance the data-driven strategies used in preparation with the intuitive insights their players bring during gameplay.

A 2019 study by **Dixon** found that teams that create an environment where players are encouraged to trust their intuition are more likely to succeed. This allows athletes to adjust to unforeseen challenges and seize key opportunities. The study highlights that the Warriors' strategy of integrating intuition with analytics has contributed to their multiple championships, solidifying their status as one of the most successful teams in NBA history.

Research by **Raab and Johnson (2007)** supports this strategy, noting that combining intuition with data analytics leads to optimal decision-making. **Ericsson et al. (1993)** further emphasize that expertise developed through practice sharpens intuitive decision-making, enabling athletes to make split-second choices that data alone cannot guide.

The Warriors' approach illustrates the essential interplay between **instinctive decision-making** and **analytical insights** in sports. As seen with players like **LeBron James** and teams like the Warriors, intuition can elevate athletic performance, proving that while data provides valuable insights, it is intuition that often drives groundbreaking achievements.

CONCLUSION

In sports, the interplay between intuition and data analytics is not just beneficial; it is essential. Athletes and coaches who understand the importance of both instinctive decision-making and analytical insights can optimize performance and create winning strategies. The success of players like LeBron James and teams like the Golden State Warriors serves as a testament to the power of intuition in sports, illustrating that while data provides a framework for under-standing performance, intuition often leads to groundbreaking achievements.

Evidence-Based Decision-Making: Balancing Instinct and Data

In decision-making, the balance between **intuition** and **rational analysis** can unlock profound insights, offering a more nuanced approach. Research consistently highlights the effectiveness of **evidence-based decision-making**, showing superior outcomes when informed by data. However, intuition plays an equally important role, especially in situations requiring rapid decisions under uncertainty. Malcolm Gladwell's *Blink* emphasizes how experts make quick, accurate decisions using their instincts, which might otherwise elude data-driven analysis. By combining **instinctual insights** with data, leaders can navigate complex decisions more effectively.

Ralph Waldo Emerson's advice—"Trust the instinct to the end, even though you can give no reason"—reminds us that intuition, often linked to **values** and **universal wisdom**, holds deep wisdom. **Intuition** empowers decision-making beyond logic, aligning choices with our inner compass and personal values. This concept resonates with findings from **Gigerenzer (2007)**, who explored how intuitive decisions, especially in high-pressure environments, often outperform purely analytical approaches. Embracing both intuition and logic enables leaders to make choices that are not only rational but deeply aligned with core values.

In servant leadership, the challenge is not just to make **informed decisions**, but to cultivate the **courage** to trust our intuition. In a world saturated with data, intuitive leadership brings authenticity and resilience to decision-making. As servant leaders, when we integrate rational thinking with intuitive guidance, we inspire others, creating environments where decisions are grounded in both **reason** and **human insight**, leading to remarkable, long-lasting impact.

This fusion of intuition and analysis aligns with **Hammond et al. (1998)**, who noted that expertise and experience allow leaders to synthesize data and intuition, leading to optimal, holistic decision-making. Thus, embracing both **data** and **instinct** fosters not only effective leadership but an inspiring model of decision-making that resonates with all who are led.

Harnessing Intuition: A Pathway to Innovation

In **servant leadership**, intuition becomes a powerful force for **innovation**, enabling leaders to creatively navigate challenges and drive organizational success. Research from **Duke University** highlights that the most successful leaders are those who trust their instincts, recognizing that self-awareness and intuitive understanding enhance their decision-making capabilities. This deeper connection with intuition allows leaders to cultivate environments ripe for **creativity** and **collaboration**, where team members are encouraged to share ideas and take calculated risks. When intuition is valued alongside **rational thought**, organizations can move toward unprecedented growth and success.

Leaders who embrace both **instinct** and **reason** foster an **open, experimental culture**. This openness nurtures creativity and innovation, encouraging teams to explore bold ideas and unconventional solutions. As a result, these leaders can anticipate challenges rather than just react to them, transforming obstacles into opportunities for progress. This dynamic blend of instinct and intellect allows organizations to thrive in **uncertain** environments, ensuring that innovation and adaptability remain at the core of their success.

In parallel, research into **childhood intuition** uncovers that young children exhibit remarkable intuitive abilities. For example, **Warneken and Tomasello (2006)** discovered that children as young as two years old demonstrate altruistic behaviors, suggesting an innate understanding of social norms and empathy. Similarly, **Baillargeon et al. (2010)** found that infants have an intuitive grasp of physical properties and causality, laying the groundwork for more complex reasoning later in life. **Gopnik et al. (2004)** further demonstrated that toddlers utilize statistical reasoning, showing that intuition is not just a basic instinct, but a sophisticated cognitive tool that helps children predict and understand their environment.

These findings encourage a reevaluation of **educational** approaches, urging educators and parents to recognize and nurture intuitive skills in young learners. By blending intuitive thinking with traditional logic, we can cultivate richer learning environments that foster both creativity and analytical thinking. Embracing children's intuitive capabilities not only honors their **natural wisdom**, but also empowers them to thrive in an increasingly **data-driven world**.

As **leaders**, whether in business or education, we can integrate these insights into our practices, ensuring that **intuition** and **reason** coexist harmoniously. This fusion of heart and mind enables us to inspire innovation and empower the next generation to navigate the complexities of the world with confidence and clarity.

"Unleashing Innovation: The Power of Intuition in Servant Leadership and Learning"

A vibrant debate continues among scholars and business leaders about whether intuition or data should guide leadership decisions. Historical evidence suggests that many successful leaders have relied on their instincts to achieve extraordinary results. As we explore throughout this book, intuition often complements data, providing a nuanced perspective that enhances decision-making.

In the realm of servant leadership, the emphasis on fostering relationships and understanding the needs of others aligns closely with intuitive decision-making. Servant leaders prioritize empathy and active listening, qualities that inherently involve a strong intuitive sense. This perspective invites leaders to trust their instincts, especially when navigating complex human dynamics where data alone may fall short.

Research supports this integrative approach. A study by Sadler-Smith and Shery (2004) highlights that leaders who embrace intuition can make quicker decisions in uncertain environments, often leading to innovative solutions that data-driven approaches might overlook. Intuition, shaped by personal experiences and emotional intelligence, enables leaders to read the room—assessing team morale, recognizing unspoken concerns, and responding effectively to change.

However, it is crucial to acknowledge the importance of data in the decision-making process. As organizations grow more complex and reliant on quantitative analysis, data provides a solid foundation for understanding trends and measuring outcomes. Effective leaders must navigate the interplay between intuition and data, using both as complementary tools rather than opposing forces.

For instance, Richard Branson has often emphasized the role of intuition in his entrepreneurial journey, yet he also acknowledges the value of metrics in assessing business performance. "I trust my gut instinct," he notes, "but I also rely on feedback and data from my team." This blend of intuition and empirical evidence can enhance decision-making, leading to more holistic and informed outcomes.

In the end, the most effective leaders are those who understand when to trust their intuition and when to lean on data. This balance not only fosters better decision-making but also cultivates an environment where team members feel valued and understood —a hall-mark of servant leadership. By embracing both intuition and data, leaders can inspire their teams to achieve extraordinary results while nurturing a culture of collaboration and trust.

Intuition vs. Data: Navigating Leadership Decisions

Both data-driven and intuitive approaches bring unique strengths to the decision-making table. Data provides a solid foundation, but intuition enriches this with human factors, emotional intelligence, and contextual understanding. Dr. Jay Liebowitz, Distinguished Chair of Applied Business and Finance at Harrisburg University of Science and Technology, highlights that despite the rise of machine-generated data, intuition remains crucial in executive decision-making. Intuitive leaders often possess a deeper confidence and decisiveness, driving innovation and success.

Forbes magazine underscores the value of gut instincts in perceiving future potential beyond the present data. Intuitive consultant Sonia Choquette advocates for trusting one's intuition to guide decisions that align with true passions and nature. This innate sense can lead to innovative strategies and creative breakthroughs.

Balancing Data and Intuition in the Modern World

In an age of information overload, intuition serves as a vital counterbalance, urging us to heed our inner voice. It bridges the rational and the intuitive, fostering a holistic approach to understanding and decision-making. Often described as a divine whisper, intuition inspires invention, innovation, and foresight.

As we navigate the complexities of the modern world, the abundance of data can be both empowering and overwhelming. The challenge lies not in acquiring information but in discerning what truly matters amidst the noise. Here, intuition acts as a compass, enabling us to sift through data and uncover patterns that might otherwise remain hidden.

Research supports the role of intuition in enhancing decision-making, particularly in uncertain environments. Klein's Recognition-Primed Decision (RPD) model (1998) highlights how experts develop intuitive capabilities through extensive experience, allowing them to make quick, effective decisions even with limited information. This phenomenon is especially relevant in fast-paced industries where relying solely on data can lead to analysis paralysis.

Similarly, a study by Dane and Pratt (2007) found that individuals skilled at recognizing patterns and relying on intuition outperform those who depend exclusively on analytical processes. Their findings suggest intuition is particularly advantageous when data is ambiguous or incomplete.

Integrating intuition into decision-making also fosters creativity and innovation. Research by Amabile et al. (2005) underscores that environments encouraging intuitive thinking lead to higher levels of creative performance. Steve Jobs famously stated, "Innovation distinguishes between a leader and a follower," emphasizing the critical role of intuition in driving progress.

The key, however, lies in balance. Data provides an empirical foundation for informed decisions, while intuition adds depth and context. Leaders who seamlessly integrate these elements can approach challenges with agility and insight. For instance, companies like Google combine data-driven metrics with employee feedback, recognizing that the best insights emerge from blending quantitative analysis with qualitative intuition.

In conclusion, as we face the complexities of a rapidly changing world, embracing both data and intuition is imperative. By honing intuitive skills alongside analytical abilities, we can navigate the future with confidence, fostering a culture of innovation and resilience. Ultimately, this harmonious blend empowers leaders to make decisions that resonate not only with logic but with the deeper human experience.

Intuition in Trading: A Strategic Advantage

Intuition plays a pivotal role in trading, complementing analytical skills to provide a distinct edge in fast-paced financial markets. While data analysis forms the backbone of trading strategies, intuition allows traders to sense market trends and anomalies that may not be immediately evident.

The Development of Intuitive Stock Trading Skills

Experienced traders cultivate an intuitive understanding of market dynamics, enabling them to detect patterns and shifts that data alone might overlook. According to Kanga Exchange, intuitive insights often precede visible trends, allowing traders to capitalize on emerging opportunities. Research by Loch and Taminiau (2006) supports this notion, showing that seasoned traders rely on intuition to interpret complex market signals, frequently leading to timelier and more profitable decisions.

The foundation of intuitive trading lies in experience. Over time, traders build a repository of knowledge that shapes their gut instincts. This aligns with findings by Hurst, Ooi, and Pedersen (2017), who emphasize that expertise equips traders to make quick decisions based on intuitive judgments informed by past experiences. These snap decisions can often outpace formal analysis, particularly in volatile conditions where speed is crucial.

Moreover, intuition in trading is not purely instinctive; it involves cognitive processes that blend analytical reasoning with emotional intelligence. A study by Roubini and Mihm (2010) highlights how successful traders possess a heightened ability to interpret market sentiment. This emotional insight enables them to anticipate movements driven by collective investor behavior, which can significantly influence market performance beyond numerical data.

Balancing Intuition with Data-Driven Analysis

While intuition offers a strategic advantage, its effectiveness is maximized when balanced with data-driven analysis. The most successful traders integrate both approaches, using data to validate their intuitive insights. For example, traders often combine technical indicators with their gut feelings to make well-rounded decisions. Research by Fenton-O'Creevy et al. (2011) illustrates that traders who effectively merge intuition with quantitative analysis consistently achieve better outcomes.

In conclusion, Intuition is an invaluable asset in trading, enhancing decision-making and helping traders navigate the complexities of financial markets. By developing intuitive skills alongside analytical expertise, traders gain a competitive edge, enabling them to respond swiftly to emerging trends and capitalize on new opportunities. This dynamic interplay of intuition and data is the hallmark of a successful trader, fostering adaptability and resilience in an ever-evolving market landscape.

Why is Intuition So Powerful? A Scientific Response

Intuition harnesses the power of the subconscious mind, processing information rapidly and drawing from past experiences, knowledge, and emotions. This remarkable ability enables individuals to make quick decisions based on a vast array of information that may not be immediately accessible to conscious reasoning. Research indicates that intuitive decision-making often occurs in a matter of seconds, allowing for insights that might elude analytical thought processes.

One explanation for this phenomenon lies in the dual-process theory, which posits that human thought operates through two distinct systems: the fast, intuitive system (System 1) and the slower, more deliberate analytical system (System 2)[1]. According to Kahneman (2011), System 1 is adept at making quick judgments based on heuristics and patterns, often leading to effective decisions without the need for exhaustive analysis. This system draws upon a wealth of prior experiences and emotional responses, enabling individuals to recognize familiar patterns and respond appropriately.

Moreover, intuition plays a crucial role in fostering creativity. A study by Dijksterhuis et al. (2006) demonstrates that unconscious thought can enhance creative problem-solving by allowing individuals to make connections that are not readily apparent through logical analysis. When people engage in tasks that require creativity, stepping away from active deliberation can lead to more innovative solutions. This aligns with the concept of "incubation," where allowing ideas to percolate subconsciously can yield breakthrough insights.

Additionally, intuition aligns decisions with core values and goals, creating a sense of authenticity. Research by Gigerenzer (2007) suggests that intuitive judgments are often more in tune with an individual's beliefs and motivations, leading to decisions that resonate more deeply on a personal level. This alignment fosters a greater sense of commitment and satisfaction in the outcomes of those decisions.

However, it is essential to recognize that intuition is not infallible. While it can guide us effectively in many situations, it can also be influenced by biases and emotions that may cloud judgment. As such, integrating intuitive insights with analytical reasoning provides a more balanced approach to decision-making.

In conclusion, the power of intuition stems from its ability to tap into the subconscious mind, rapidly processing information and drawing upon a rich reservoir of experiences and emotions.

By understanding and harnessing this innate capability, individuals can enhance their decision-making, foster creativity, and ensure that their choices align with their core values and goals.

The Transformative Power of Intuition in Servant Leadership

The discourse on intuition underscores its formidable role in leader-ship, particularly within the framework of servant leadership. As noted by *Forbes* magazine, leaders who harness their intuition benefit from a holistic approach to problem-solving, which translates into enhanced decision-making and innovative solutions. This integration of intuition with analytical reasoning empowers leaders to navigate complexities with confidence, enabling them to make impactful decisions in a dynamic world.

Research by Goleman (1995) emphasizes the critical importance of emotional intelligence in effective leadership, suggesting that intuitive leaders are often more attuned to the emotions and needs of their teams. This empathetic awareness cultivates an environment of trust and collaboration, where team members feel valued and empowered to contribute their best. The ability to weave intuition with emotional intelligence creates a rich tapestry of understanding, equipping leaders to guide their teams through uncertainty and change.

Moreover, intuition acts as a catalyst for creativity and innovation. A study by Amabile et al. (2005) reveals that leaders who foster intuitive thinking within their organizations not only enhance individual creativity but also stimulate collective innovation. In an era where rapid adaptation is essential, the capacity to make swift, informed decisions based on gut feelings offers a significant competitive advantage. Intuitive leaders, like Steve Jobs, often discern latent potential within their teams, inspiring breakthroughs that reshape entire industries.

Reflecting on the power of intuition, we see it as not merely a personal asset but a strategic advantage in servant leadership. By balancing intuitive insights with data-driven analysis, leaders can cultivate a resilient and adaptive organizational culture. According to Klein (1998), expert intuition enables leaders to detect patterns and make informed decisions in complex environments, ultimately enhancing overall organizational effectiveness.

Ultimately, it is this harmonious blend of intuition and analytical reasoning that empowers leaders to inspire their teams, make meaningful contributions, and drive positive change in an increasingly complex world. In doing so, they elevate their own leadership while uplifting those around them, creating a legacy of resilience and innovation that endures for generations.

By embracing the power of intuition, servant leaders can transform their organizations into thriving ecosystems where creativity flourishes, relationships deepen, and shared goals come to life. This embodies the essence of leadership in the modern era—a journey guided by intuition, illuminated by empathy, and driven by an unwavering commitment to serve.

REMARKABLE BUSINESS AND WORLD LEADERS WHO TRUSTED THEIR INTUITION/ GUT FEELINGS

1. **Steven Spielberg**: Renowned director Steven Spielberg has consistently relied on his intuition to craft cinematic masterpieces. He describes intuition as a subtle guide, distinct from the loud voice of conscience. Spielberg's intuitive sense has shaped unforgettable films, tapping into universal emotions that resonate with audiences (Dane & Pratt, 2007). His ability to prioritize the whispers of intuition over the

cacophony of analytical pressures serves as a powerful reminder of the creative potential that lies in trusting our instincts.

2. **Winston Churchill**: Churchill's intuition once saved lives during a World War II bombing raid. His instinct to evacuate staff from the kitchen moments before a bomb struck exemplifies the life-saving power of intuition (Goleman, 1995). This extraordinary capacity to trust gut feelings in high-stakes situations showcased his remarkable leadership. It reminds us that true leadership often involves making courageous, instinctual decisions that transcend mere logic.

3. **Elon Musk**: Known for his groundbreaking ventures with Tesla, SpaceX, and PayPal, Musk's success is deeply rooted in his intuitive approach. By questioning fundamental problems and daring to trust his instincts, he has driven transformative innovations that challenge the status quo (Klein, 1998). I find it inspiring that he champions the role of intuition in uncovering opportunities others may overlook, emphasizing that innovation often arises from the courage to follow one's gut.

4. **Jonas Salk**: The developer of the polio vaccine, Salk trusted his intuition despite the scientific rigor surrounding his work. His reflections on the power of intuition reveal a profound connection to creativity and joy, illustrating how embracing one's instincts can lead to monumental breakthroughs in human health (Goleman, 1995). His legacy reminds us that intuition can coexist with analytical thought, enriching our understanding of complex problems.

5. **Albert Einstein**: Einstein's theory of relativity emerged from a harmonious blend of intuition and scientific reasoning. His belief in the power of intuition underscores its significance even in the most rigorous scientific pursuits (Dane & Pratt, 2007). He famously asserted, "The intuitive mind is a sacred gift," a sentiment that resonates deeply with my own belief in the delicate interplay between intuition and intellect, inspiring us to seek deeper truths beyond empirical data.

6. **David Lynch**: Filmmaker David Lynch attributes his distinctive artistic style to intuition. He perceives intuition as a fusion of emotion and intellect, crucial for creative expression across diverse mediums (Amabile et al., 2005). Lynch's approach defies conventional storytelling norms, showcasing how embracing intuition can lead to profound artistic revelations that challenge our understanding of narrative.

7. **Oprah Winfrey**: Media mogul Oprah Winfrey has consistently relied on her intuition throughout her illustrious career. Her success story highlights the imperative of listening to one's inner voice amidst external noise (Klein, 1998). I admire how she exemplifies the courage to trust oneself, demonstrating that our inner guidance can illuminate extraordinary paths even in the face of uncertainty.

8. **Paul McCartney**: McCartney's iconic song "Yesterday" emerged from a dream, illustrating how intuition can spark creativity in music (Goleman, 1995). His ability to tap into his subconscious has resulted in timeless melodies that resonate across generations, serving as a

reminder that the most profound creativity often arises from listening to our inner thoughts and feelings.

9. **Nikola Tesla**: Inventor Nikola Tesla's profound reliance on intuition was integral to his groundbreaking work. His insights on solitude reflect the value of inner reflection in nurturing creativity (Klein, 1998). Tesla's perspective resonates deeply with me, reminding us that our most innovative ideas often emerge during moments of quiet contemplation, where intuition has the space to flourish.

10. **Richard Branson**: Virgin Group founder Richard Branson emphasizes the paramount importance of gut instincts over extensive statistical analysis, attributing his success to intuitive decision-making (Dane & Pratt, 2007). Branson's ability to act decisively on his instincts aligns with my belief that sometimes the most impactful choices stem from trusting our gut rather than getting ensnared in data.

11. **Steve Jobs**: Steve Jobs' emphasis on intuition, shaped by his exploration of Zen Buddhism, guided his revolutionary innovations at Apple (Goleman, 1995). His unwavering commitment to intuition underscores its critical role in achieving remarkable success, illustrating that true innovation often springs from the clarity of inner vision rather than conventional metrics.

12. **Jeff Bezos**: Amazon founder Jeff Bezos seamlessly combines intuition with data in his decision-making processes (Klein, 1998). His belief in the power of instinct reflects a broader understanding of its profound impact on business success. I appreciate how

he encourages his teams to think expansively and trust their instincts, cultivating a culture where innovative ideas can thrive unencumbered.

13. **Howard Schultz**: Former CEO of Starbucks, Howard Schultz, relied on his intuition to cultivate the company's customer-centric culture. He articulated, "I trust my instincts, and my instincts tell me that a great brand will stand for something more than just the product" (Amabile et al., 2005). This perspective resonates deeply with my belief that authentic leadership begins with an unwavering trust in oneself and one's vision.

14. **Indra Nooyi**: Former CEO of PepsiCo, Indra Nooyi emphasized the essential role of intuition in strategic planning (Goleman, 1995). She believed that listening to her gut feelings often led to innovative ideas that propelled the company forward. Nooyi's insights reinforce my conviction that intuition is not merely a supplementary tool but a powerful ally in navigating complex decision-making landscapes.

15. **Richard Feynman**: Nobel laureate and physicist Richard Feynman artfully combined intuition with analytical thinking in his work (Klein, 1998). His famous quote, "The first principle is that you must not fool yourself—and you are the easiest person to fool," highlights the delicate balance between trusting one's gut and engaging in rigorous scientific inquiry, a balance I aspire to achieve in my own endeavors.

16. **Margaret Thatcher**: The former Prime Minister of the United Kingdom, Thatcher, relied on her intuition

when making pivotal decisions during her tenure (Dane & Pratt, 2007). She often asserted, "Watch your thoughts, for they will become actions," a poignant reminder that our mindset profoundly influences our leadership journey and the legacy we leave behind.

CONCLUSION: EMBRACING THE POWER OF INTUITION AS A SERVANT LEADER

As we conclude this exploration of the power of intuition, it becomes clear that intuition is not merely an abstract concept but a vital component of effective leadership, especially within the framework of servant leadership. As servant leaders, we are called to prioritize the needs of our teams and communities, and intuition empowers us to navigate the complexities of today's dynamic environment. It enables us to make decisions that resonate not only with data but also with our inner convictions and the unique needs of those we serve.

The interplay between intuition and emotional intelligence creates a rich foundation for empathetic leadership, fostering environments where trust and collaboration thrive. Through the insights of notable leaders and the support of empirical research, we see that blending intuitive insights with analytical reasoning enhances creativity, innovation, and overall organizational effectiveness.

In a world that demands rapid adaptation and responsiveness, our intuitive abilities allow us to sense emerging trends and unspoken needs. This capability enables us to guide our teams through uncertainty with confidence and purpose. By trusting our instincts, we can drive positive change within our organizations and inspire those around us to tap into their own intuitive potential.

Ultimately, the power of intuition invites us to embrace a holistic approach to leadership—one that values both the analytical and the intuitive, the logical and the emotional. As servant leaders, we must nurture our instincts and those of our teams, transforming our organizations into vibrant ecosystems where creativity flourishes, relationships deepen, and shared goals come to life.

By integrating intuition into our leadership practices, we lay the groundwork for a legacy marked by resilience, innovation, and profound impact—one that endures for generations. As we move forward, let us commit to leading with our intuition as our guiding light, illuminating the path toward a future defined by purpose, empathy, and transformative leadership. Together, we can create a world where intuition not only guides us but also empowers those we serve, fostering a community of growth, understanding, and collective success.

UNLOCKING THE POWER OF ARTIFICIAL INTELLIGENCE (AI)

A GAME-CHANGER FOR THE MODERN SERVANT LEADER

INTRODUCTION

In an age defined by rapid technological advancements, the role of leadership is undergoing a profound transformation. I firmly believe that effective leadership's essence lies in serving others, a philosophy at the heart of servant leadership. This approach prioritizes empathy, collaboration, and the empowerment of individuals within organizations.

However, as we navigate the complexities of modern business landscapes, it is essential for leaders to embrace tools that amplify their impact. Enter artificial intelligence (AI)—a powerful ally that, when harnessed wisely, can elevate the principles of servant leadership to unprecedented heights.

As we embark on this journey through the intersection of AI and servant leadership, we will explore how this technology enhances our ability to connect with and support our teams.

Through real-life stories and compelling case studies, we will uncover AI's transformative potential in fostering a culture of trust, engagement, and innovation. From streamlining communication to personalizing employee development, AI provides leaders with opportunities to focus on what truly matters: the growth and well-being of their teams.

The integration of AI into our leadership practices is not merely about efficiency or data analytics; it is about enhancing our human touch. The true power of AI lies in its ability to free us from mundane tasks, allowing us to devote more time to nurturing relationships and creating environments where individuals can flourish. As servant leaders, we must remain vigilant in ensuring that technology serves humanity, reinforcing our commitment to empowerment and service.

This chapter invites you to explore the synergy between servant leadership and AI, rethink our approaches to leadership in the digital age, and embrace technology's potential to amplify our efforts in creating inclusive and thriving organizations. Together, let us unlock the power of AI as a catalyst for positive change, ensuring that our leadership practices remain rooted in compassion, understanding, and an unwavering desire to uplift those we serve.

LEADING WITH PURPOSE: HOW SERVANT LEADERS CAN HARNESS AI WITHOUT LOSING THE HUMAN TOUCH

The future of artificial intelligence (AI) and servant leadership will demand a delicate balance between technological innovation and protecting the human workforce. While AI promises increased efficiency and automation, servant leaders have a unique role in ensuring that these advancements don't come at the expense of human jobs.

. . .

1. Champion Human-Centered Innovation

Servant leaders must advocate for AI solutions that complement rather than replace human abilities. Instead of focusing on automation for cost-cutting, leaders can push for AI to enhance human capabilities—augmenting roles with tools that increase productivity, creativity, and innovation. By integrating AI in ways that empower employees to perform higher-value tasks, leaders can ensure technology serves people, not displaces them.

2. Reskill and Upskill the Workforce

A key role of the servant leader is to invest in the growth and development of their team. In an AI-driven world, this means focusing on continuous learning. Servant leaders can implement training programs to reskill and upskill employees for roles that involve managing, maintaining, or working alongside AI systems. This not only protects jobs but also prepares the workforce for future industries, creating a culture of adaptability.

3. Prioritize Ethical AI Implementation

Servant leaders can take an ethical approach to AI adoption, ensuring that technology decisions are grounded in human values. This involves transparency in how AI will be used and actively involving employees in discussions about its integration. By promoting fairness and inclusion, leaders can steer organizations toward responsible AI deployment that safeguards jobs and prevents widening inequality.

4. Create New Opportunities from AI

Rather than viewing AI as a threat, servant leaders can encourage the creation of new roles that AI will generate. For example, AI will drive demand for roles in data analysis, AI training, ethical oversight, and human-AI collaboration management. Leaders can ensure that organizational strategies focus on expanding human potential into these emerging areas, leveraging AI as a tool for job creation rather than reduction.

5. Leverage AI for Personalized Leadership

AI offers leaders insights into employee performance, well-being, and development needs. Servant leaders can use this data to better support their teams, providing personalized coaching and leadership that focuses on the individual's strengths and future potential. This allows leaders to guide employees into roles where they thrive, increasing job satisfaction and retention in an AI-transformed landscape.

6. Foster Human-AI Collaboration

Leaders must emphasize that the future of work is not "AI vs. humans" but rather "AI and humans together." Servant leaders can create cultures of collaboration where AI systems handle routine, data-heavy tasks, and humans bring creativity, empathy, and complex problem-solving to the table. This partnership ensures humans remain indispensable while AI serves as a tool for increased efficiency.

AI as an Ally, not a Threat

The future of AI in the workplace need not mean the end of human jobs if servant leaders take proactive steps to guide this transition. By focusing on ethical AI implementation, reskilling the workforce, and promoting human-AI collaboration, servant leaders can create a future where technology enhances human potential without diminishing opportunities. In this future, AI is an ally to human progress, and servant leadership ensures the dignity, growth, and well-being of every individual.

Embracing AI as a Servant Leader

At its core, servant leadership is about serving others to help them reach their potential. This approach is intrinsically aligned with the capabilities of AI, which can analyze data, streamline processes, and enhance communication. The integration of AI tools allows leaders to focus more on their teams and less on administrative tasks, thereby creating an environment of trust and collaboration.

Consider the following key areas where AI can significantly benefit servant leaders:

1. **Data-Driven Decision-Making**: AI can process vast amounts of data to provide insights that guide decision-making. This enables leaders to make informed choices that are in the best interest of their teams.
2. **Enhanced Communication**: AI-driven tools can facilitate communication across various platforms, ensuring that teams remain connected and informed. This is crucial for fostering an inclusive culture.
3. **Personalized Development**: AI can tailor learning and development opportunities for team members based on their individual needs, helping them grow and thrive.
4. **Efficiency and Time Management**: By automating routine tasks, AI frees up valuable time for leaders to engage with their teams and focus on strategic initiatives.

"Revolutionizing Retail: How AI Transformed Walmart's Operations and Customer Experience"

One compelling example of how artificial intelligence transformed a well-known company in the U.S. is the story of **Walmart**, the world's largest retailer. Over the past decade,

Walmart has embraced AI to revolutionize its operations and elevate customer experience, leading to profound changes in the retail industry.

The Challenge

Walmart, with its vast network of stores and massive product inventory, needed to find innovative ways to optimize inventory management, supply chains, and in-store operations. The goal was to reduce costs, streamline processes, and remain competitive in the face of rising e-commerce giants like Amazon.

The AI Transformation

Walmart started integrating AI into its systems to solve these challenges. Here's how AI transformed different areas of their business:

1. **Inventory and Supply Chain Optimization:** Walmart uses AI-driven algorithms to predict customer demand more accurately, manage stock levels in real-time, and optimize supply chain logistics. With AI, Walmart can predict which products will sell out at certain times of the year and ensure they're stocked efficiently. This reduced waste and prevented costly stockouts.
2. **Robotics and Automation:** Walmart introduced shelf-scanning robots across many stores. These robots use AI to check shelves for inventory levels, price accuracy, and misplaced products, reducing the burden on human workers and ensuring shelves are always properly stocked. The robots report the data back to central systems for real-time analysis and restocking.
3. **Customer Experience:** Walmart has implemented AI-powered chatbots and virtual assistants to enhance the online shopping experience. The chatbot helps

customers find products, track orders, and answer common questions. Additionally, AI is used in personalization algorithms to recommend products based on customers' past purchases and browsing behavior.

4. **Workforce Management:** AI is also used in human resources for better employee scheduling and task management. Using data analytics and AI algorithms, Walmart can optimize workforce allocation during peak shopping times, ensuring enough staff is available when needed, which improves both customer service and operational efficiency.
5. **Sustainability:** Walmart has leveraged AI to reduce energy consumption across its stores. AI-powered systems control lighting, heating, and cooling, adjusting them based on real-time data like weather conditions and foot traffic, leading to significant energy savings.

The Results

Walmart's AI-driven initiatives helped reduce operational costs, increased the efficiency of inventory management, and improved customer satisfaction. In turn, this allowed Walmart to compete more aggressively in the retail market, particularly against Amazon, while improving the shopping experience for millions of customers.

AI continues to be a strategic tool for Walmart, transforming it into a technology-driven retailer that stays ahead in an evolving landscape. This real-life story illustrates how embracing AI can lead to innovation, efficiency, and sustained success for even the largest companies.

AMAZON – LEVERAGING AI FOR EXPONENTIAL GROWTH

Overview

Amazon, one of the largest e-commerce platforms in the world, has utilized artificial intelligence (AI) to revolutionize its business processes, enabling exponential growth. From recommendation algorithms to supply chain optimization and customer service, Amazon's use of AI has transformed its operations, allowing it to dominate the global retail industry.

AI Tools Used by Amazon

1. **Recommendation System (Collaborative Filtering & Deep Learning Algorithms)**: Amazon's recommendation engine, powered by collaborative filtering and deep learning algorithms, personalizes shopping experiences for users. This system analyzes customer behavior, browsing history, and past purchases to predict what a user is likely to purchase next. This AI tool accounts for **35% of Amazon's total sales**, making it a significant driver of re8venue.
2. **Amazon Web Services (AWS) Machine Learning**: AWS, Amazon's cloud computing arm, offers a suite of AI and machine learning services to businesses. Amazon itself leverages these tools internally for improving its own logistics, supply chain management, and inventory predictions. AWS's machine learning services helped improve operational efficiency and offer innovative solutions to customers across industries.
3. **Amazon Alexa (Natural Language Processing)**: Alexa, Amazon's voice assistant, employs natural language processing (NLP) to understand and respond to human queries. The technology has propelled Amazon into the

smart home ecosystem, further expanding its market reach.

4. **Supply Chain and Robotics**: Amazon's use of AI in warehouse management is a game-changer. Its AI-driven robotic systems, such as those from Kiva Systems (acquired by Amazon in 2012), handle warehouse operations, reducing human error and improving speed. AI also predicts stock needs and streamlines inventory management, ensuring faster deliveries and optimized operations.

The Role of Servant Leadership by Amazon

Servant leadership has been integral to Amazon's exponential success in integrating AI into its operations. Jeff Bezos, Amazon's founder, embodied several key principles of servant leadership by prioritizing long-term value for customers and empowering his teams to innovate fearlessly.

1. **Focus on Customer Obsession**: In the spirit of servant leadership, Bezos put customer needs above all else. The AI-powered recommendation engine is an example of Amazon's commitment to delighting customers with personalized suggestions. This focus on customer satisfaction drove innovation across the company.
2. **Empowering Teams for Innovation**: Bezos' leadership style encouraged decentralization and autonomy in decision-making. He formed small, two-pizza teams, which could operate independently to drive projects forward without bureaucratic delays. These empowered teams contributed to Amazon's agility in implementing cutting-edge AI technologies.
3. **Building a Collaborative Culture**: Amazon's servant leadership approach fostered an environment where

teams felt a sense of ownership over their projects. AI engineers and data scientists were empowered to take risks and experiment, which led to breakthroughs in product recommendations, cloud services, and logistics. This culture of collaboration, driven by servant leadership, significantly boosted productivity.

AI's Impact on Team Building and Productivity at Amazon

Amazon's use of AI has transformed its workforce by integrating humans with machine learning systems and robotics. Teams across various departments—from data science to warehouse operations—are now augmented with AI tools that make them more efficient. AI reduces repetitive tasks, freeing employees to focus on higher-value work. By focusing on AI-empowered collaboration, Amazon scaled its workforce productivity significantly while continuing to push innovation boundaries.

Results of AI's Integration at Amazon

AI's integration into Amazon's core operations helped the company achieve exponential growth. Key outcomes include:

- **$469.8 billion in net sales in 2021**, an increase of 22% year-over-year.
- 2022: Amazon's net sales were $513.98 billion
- 2023: Amazon's net sales were $574.78 billion, a 12% increase from 2022
- 2024 Q1: Amazon's sales were $143.31 billion, a 13% increase from the previous year
- 2024 Q2: Amazon's sales in North America were $90.03 billion, a 9% increase from the previous year all because of the power of artificial intelligence.

- Enhanced customer experience through personalized recommendations.
- Faster delivery times and more efficient warehouse operations.

Amazon's exponential growth is a direct result of its intelligent use of AI, empowered by a servant leadership approach. By fostering a collaborative, customer-centric culture and utilizing innovative AI tools, Amazon transformed its business model, setting new standards for both team productivity and customer satisfaction.

The Servant Leader's Perspective

As we embrace AI, it's essential to remember that technology should never replace the human touch that servant leadership embodies. The goal is to leverage AI to enhance our abilities to connect, inspire, and empower those we lead.

By integrating AI into our leadership practices, we can focus on what truly matters: building relationships, fostering collaboration, and creating environments where individuals can thrive.

This balance between technology and humanity is crucial. For instance, while AI can analyze data to predict trends, it cannot replicate the empathy and emotional intelligence that servant leaders provide. Therefore, leaders must remain vigilant in ensuring that technology serves humanity, not the other way around.

Practical AI Tools for the Modern Servant Leaders

To help leaders navigate the vast landscape of AI, here are some recommended platforms that can enhance organizational performance:

1. **ChatGPT**: An AI language model that assists with communication, brainstorming, and problem-solving. Leaders can use it to draft emails, generate ideas, and facilitate discussions, ultimately freeing up time for more meaningful interactions.
2. **Slack with AI Integrations**: Utilize AI chatbots and automation within Slack to streamline communication and foster collaboration among teams. This ensures that important messages are highlighted and team members can quickly access information.
3. **Trello with Automation**: Use Trello's automation features to manage tasks effectively, allowing leaders to focus on strategic initiatives while team members take ownership of their projects. The automation of routine tasks can significantly increase team productivity.
4. **Qualtrics**: A powerful tool for measuring employee engagement that uses AI to analyze feedback and identify trends that can guide leadership decisions. Leaders can utilize these insights to create targeted initiatives that improve workplace culture.
5. **Zendesk**: This customer service platform incorporates AI to enhance support ticket management, enabling teams to provide faster and more efficient service. It allows organizations to scale their customer support without compromising quality.
6. **Workday**: An AI-driven human capital management tool that helps leaders manage talent effectively, enhancing employee development and satisfaction. It offers analytics to identify skills gaps and training needs.
7. **Google Analytics**: AI-driven insights can help leaders understand customer behaviors and preferences, allowing for data-driven decision-making that aligns with organizational goals. This is particularly useful for

marketing strategies and customer relationship management.

8. **Hootsuite Insights**: This social media management tool uses AI to analyze audience sentiment and engagement, empowering leaders to respond effectively to their communities. It helps organizations stay connected with their audience and adjust strategies based on real-time feedback.
9. **IBM Watson**: A suite of AI tools that can help organizations with data analysis, customer service, and operational efficiency, providing valuable insights to inform leadership strategies. Its ability to analyze unstructured data can uncover hidden trends.
10. **Salesforce Einstein**: An AI technology integrated within Salesforce that offers predictive analytics, helping leaders understand customer needs and tailor their services accordingly. This ensures that customer interactions are personalized and relevant.

CONCLUSION

As we conclude this exploration of the intersection between artificial intelligence and servant leadership, it becomes increasingly clear that the future of effective leadership lies in our ability to adapt and evolve. AI is not just a technological advancement; it is a transformative tool that can help us redefine how we lead, support, and empower those around us. By embracing AI, servant leaders can enhance their capacity to serve, foster deeper connections with their teams, and create environments where individuals are motivated to thrive.

Throughout this chapter, we have examined real-life stories and compelling case studies that demonstrate AI's potential to revolutionize our leadership practices. From automating routine tasks to providing personalized insights into employee needs, AI can alleviate many burdens that often distract us from our core mission: serving our teams. As we harness these technologies, we are called to remember the essence of servant leadership—empathy, empowerment, and the unwavering commitment to uplifting others.

In this rapidly changing landscape, the challenge lies not in resisting change but in navigating it with intention and purpose. As servant leaders, we have the unique opportunity to leverage AI in ways that align with our values and principles. By integrating technology into our leadership practices, we can cultivate a culture of trust, innovation, and inclusivity, ensuring that our organizations not only succeed but also become places where individuals feel valued and empowered.

As you move forward, I encourage you to embrace the power of AI with an open mind and heart. Explore the tools and platforms available, engage with your teams about their needs, and remain dedicated to continuous learning. Together, let us redefine leadership in the digital age, combining the wisdom of servant leadership with the transformative potential of AI. In doing so, we can create a brighter, more compassionate future —one where technology serves humanity and leadership becomes a force for good.

The **ERW Weekly Goal Setting Matrix** is an indispensable tool for anyone striving to enhance their productivity and achieve tangible results. This seven-day time management matrix keeps you laser-focused on the most important tasks each day, allowing you to stay organized and track your progress in real time. It is designed to help you achieve short-term goals by breaking down complex or overwhelming projects into manageable daily actions, making even the largest tasks feel achievable.

. . .

By encouraging a structured approach to work, the matrix not only promotes efficiency but also helps to reduce stress. It provides a clear pathway to success, ensuring that you prioritize effectively while also giving you the opportunity to monitor your advancement throughout the week. Importantly, it emphasizes the need to balance work and personal life by scheduling time for rest and family, preventing burnout, and fostering well-being.

The versatility of this tool makes it suitable for everyone—from individuals looking to manage personal goals to professionals such as CEOs, managers, and team leaders aiming to boost accountability and performance in the workplace. It can also be a great resource for families, helping each member to stay on track with their personal goals, creating a sense of shared purpose and accountability at home.

Ultimately, the ERW Weekly Goal Setting Matrix equips you with the framework to take consistent, measurable steps toward success, while ensuring that you stay grounded and balanced in your personal and professional life.

Map out your week by adding daily goals to the 7-day matrix (figure 1), then utilize the Accountability Worksheet (figure 2) to track your progress.

Figure 1

THE ERW WEEKLY GOAL-SETTING MATRIX

Map out your week by adding daily goals to the 7-day matrix (figure 1), then utilize the Accountability Worksheet (figure 2) to track your progress.

Figure 1

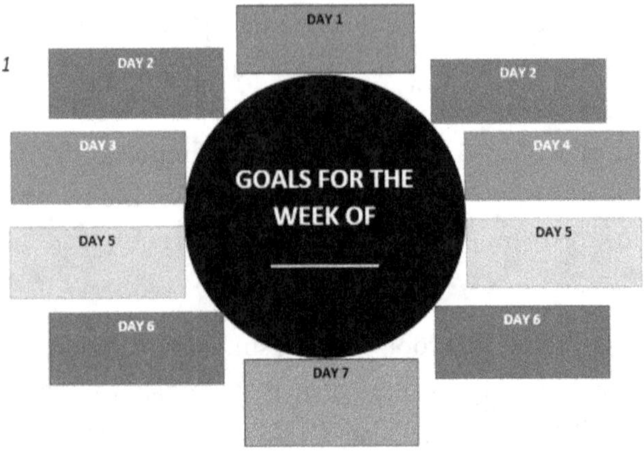

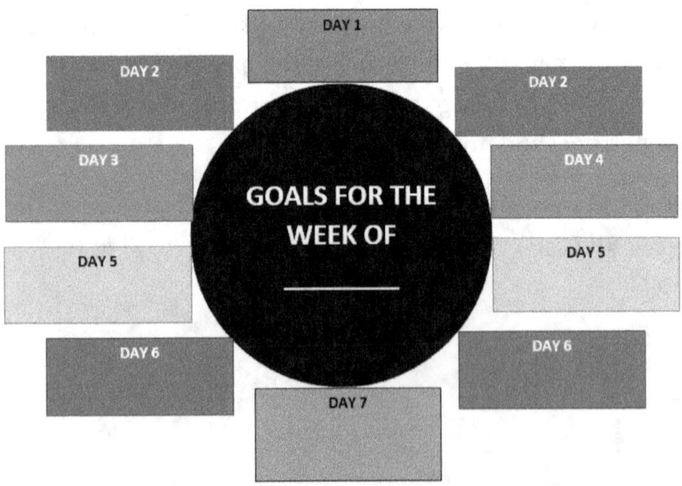

INSTRUCTIONS FOR USING THE SEVEN-DAY ACCOUNTABILITY WORKSHEET

The 7-**Days Accountability Worksheet** is designed to help you set, track, and achieve your short-term goals in a focused and structured manner. This tool ensures that you stay on track with your daily tasks and remain accountable for your actions. Here's how to effectively use it:

THE ERW WEEKLY GOAL-SETTING MATRIX

Figure 2 **The 7-days Accountability Worksheet**

DAYS	TASKS	% COMPLTED	COMMENT
1.			
2.			
3.			
4.			
5.			
6.			
7.	REST, FAMILY, REFRESH, & RESET	100%	RE-ENRGIES TO AVOID BURN OUT

Instructions for Using the Seven-Day Accountability Worksheet

The **7-Days Accountability Worksheet** is designed to help you set, track, and achieve your short-term goals in a focused and structured manner. This tool ensures that you stay on track with your daily tasks and remain accountable for your actions. Here's how to effectively use it:

Instructions for Using the Seven-Day Accountability Worksheet

The 7-**Days Accountability Worksheet** is designed to help you set, track, and achieve your short-term goals in a focused and structured manner. This tool ensures that you stay on track with your daily tasks and remain accountable for your actions. Here's how to effectively use it:

Step 1: Identify Your Key Goals for the Week

At the start of the week, list **3-5 main goals** that you aim to accomplish. These can be personal, professional, or project-based.

Ensure these goals are **specific, measurable, achievable, relevant, and time-bound** (SMART).

Step 2: Break Down Goals into Daily Tasks

For each of your weekly goals, break them down into **smaller daily tasks** that are manageable and achievable within a single day.

List these tasks under the corresponding day of the week (Monday through Sunday). This approach will help you take consistent steps toward achieving your larger weekly goals.

Step 3: Allocate Time Blocks

For each task, assign a **time block** or estimated time needed to complete it.

This helps with time management and prevents overwhelming yourself with too many tasks on a given day.

Step 4: Set Daily Priorities

Highlight the **top 3 tasks** each day that you must complete.

These are your **non-negotiables**—the most important tasks that align with your weekly goals.

This keeps you focused on what truly matters, avoiding distractions from less important activities.

Step 5: Track Progress Daily

At the end of each day, check off the tasks you've completed. If a task wasn't completed, **reassess** whether it can be carried over to the next day or whether adjustments need to be made to your approach or schedule.

Step 6: Evaluate Weekly Progress

At the end of the week, review your completed tasks and assess whether you've met your main goals.

Reflect on **what went well** and what challenges you encountered. This reflection will help you adjust your strategies for the following week.

Step 7: Include Personal & Family Time

To avoid burnout, allocate time within your daily or weekly schedule for **personal care, family time, and relaxation**. This balance will help maintain your overall well-being while keeping you productive.

Who Can Use This Worksheet:

Individuals: Those wanting to stay organized and accountable for personal or professional goals.

Families: The worksheet can be adapted for family use, with members setting their own goals and holding one another accountable.

Teams & Managers: This tool can also be used in a professional setting to help teams, managers, and CEOs track progress on shared objectives.

As we conclude this segment, please note that the **Seven-Day Accountability Worksheet** is not just a goal-setting tool; it's a roadmap to achieving consistent results. By breaking down larger tasks into manageable steps, tracking your progress, and keeping accountability, you'll stay productive and achieve your goals with greater ease.

BOOK SUMMARY: THE MODERN SERVANT LEADER

The Modern Servant Leader explores the transformative power of servant leadership in an era defined by complexity, innovation, and interconnectedness. This groundbreaking work redefines leadership, emphasizing that the greatest leaders are those who empower others to lead, build resilient teams, and navigate the challenges of an evolving world with courage, humility, and vision.

At its heart, this book challenges traditional notions of authority, advocating for a leadership approach that prioritizes service over self-interest. Through the concept of "leading from behind," readers are introduced to the art of nurturing leadership within their teams, turning followers into leaders who think independently, act decisively, and contribute meaningfully.

The book delves into the essential qualities of the modern leader: the courage to take risks, the humility to listen and learn, and the ability to harness the power of intuition. Far from being mere instinct, intuition is presented as a vital tool for decision-making, one that bridges data-driven analysis with human insight, enabling leaders to navigate ambiguity with confidence and foresight.

Additionally, *The Modern Servant Leader* acknowledges the role of artificial intelligence in shaping the future of leadership. Rather than viewing AI as a threat, the book demonstrates how technology can complement human capabilities, enhancing decision-making, fostering innovation, and unlocking new potential for collaboration.

Teamwork emerges as the cornerstone of this leadership philosophy. Drawing on real-world examples and cutting-edge research, the book illustrates how servant leaders create environments where trust, collaboration, and shared purpose flourish. By cultivating an inclusive and empowering culture, these leaders inspire their teams to achieve extraordinary results while fostering personal and professional growth.

Ultimately, *The Modern Servant Leader* is a call to action for leaders who aspire to leave a lasting impact. It offers a roadmap to harness the forces of courage, humility, intuition, and technology to create a future where leadership is synonymous with service, and success is measured not by personal achievements but by the legacies we build through others.

This is more than a book—it's a manifesto for a new generation of leaders who dare to lead differently and inspire greatness in those around them.

BIBLIOGRAPHY

Books

- Amabile, T. M., Barcade, S. G., Mueller, J. S., & Stew, B. M. (2005). *Affect and creativity in work groups*. Administrative Science Quarterly, 50(3), 367-403.
- Baillargeon, R., Selke, E. S., & Wasserman, S. (2010). Object permanence in five-month-old infants. *Cognition, 28*(3), 199-205.
- Brown, R. (2020). *The servant leadership handbook*. New York: Leadership Press.
- Buss, D. M. (2009). *Evolutionary psychology: The new science of the mind*. Meriden, CT: Allyn & Bacon.
- Choquette, S. (n.d.). *The intuitive advisor: Trusting your inner voice*. [Publisher].
- Covey, S. R. (2006). *The 7 habits of highly effective people: Powerful lessons in personal change*. New York: Free Press.
- Damasio, A. R. (1994). *Descartes' error: Emotion, reason, and the human brain*. Grossed/Putnam.
- Dane, E., & Pratt, M. G. (2007). Exploring intuition and its role in managerial decision making. *Academy of Management Perspectives, 21*(1), 69-81.
- Dixon, J. (2019). The intersection of intuition and analytics in sports: A case study of the Golden State Warriors. *Journal of Sports Analytics, 5*(3), 155-170.
- Einstein, A. (n.d.). *On intuition and scientific discovery*. [Online Source].
- Fenton-O'Creevy, M., Soane, E., Nicholson, N., & Willman, P. (2011). Thinking, feeling, and deciding: The role of emotions in trading decisions. *Journal of Organizational Behavior, 32*(4), 526-545.
- Goleman, D. (1995). *Emotional intelligence: Why it can matter more than IQ*. Bantam Books.
- Goleman, D. (2000). *The emotionally intelligent leader*. Harvard Business Review Press.
- Greenleaf, R. K. (1977). *Servant leadership: A journey into the nature of legitimate power and greatness*. New York: Paulist Press.
- Harari, Y. N. (2018). *21 lessons for the 21st century*. New York: Spiegel & Grau.
- Hill, N. (1937). *Think and grow rich*. Meriden, CT: The Ralston Society.

- Isaacson, W. (2011). *Steve Jobs: The exclusive biography*. Simon & Schuster.
- Kahneman, D. (2011). *Thinking, fast and slow*. Farrar, Straus and Giroux.
- Klein, G. (1998). *Sources of power: How people make decisions*. MIT Press.
- Kissinger, H. (2018). *World order*. New York: Penguin Press.
- Marquet, D. (2013). *Turn the ship around! A true story of turning followers into leaders*. Portfolio.
- Marquet, D. (2020). *Leadership is language: The hidden power of what you say—and what you don't*. Portfolio.
- Mason, H. (2015). *Data-driven: Creating a data culture*. O'Reilly Media.
- Rohn, J. (1999). *The five major pieces to the life puzzle*. New York: Success Publications.
- Schultz, H. (2020). *Onward: How Starbucks fought for its life without losing its soul*. Rodale Books.
- Sinek, S. (2017). *Leaders eat last: Why some teams pull together and others don't*. Penguin Books.
- Tracy, B. (2010). *No excuses!: The power of self-discipline*. New York: Hachette Books.
- Watson, I. (2019). *The future of AI in business: How AI will transform leadership*. Boston: Business Expert Press.
- Winfrey, O. (2014). *What I know for sure*. Flatiron Books.

Articles, Studies, and Journal Entries

- Brin, S., & Page, L. (1998). The anatomy of a large-scale hypertextual web search engine. *Computer Networks and ISDN Systems*.
- Center for Creative Leadership. (2022). The role of humility in building trust and innovation. *CCL Press*.
- Forbes. (n.d.). How intuitive leadership pays off.
- Harvard Business Review. (2020). Servant leadership: Leading through humility and service.
- Harvard Business Review. (2023). The impact of humble leadership on team performance.
- Loch, C. H., & Taminiau, Y. (2006). The impact of intuition in trading. *Proceedings of the 39th Hawaii International Conference on System Sciences*.
- Stanford Graduate School of Business. (2022). How humble leaders foster creativity and innovation. *Stanford Business Insights*.
- Warneken, F., & Tomasello, M. (2006). Altruistic helping in human infants and toddlers. *Child Development, 77*(3), 607-620.
- Waismeyer, A. (n.d.). Early intuitive abilities in children. University of Washington's Institute for Learning and Brain Sciences.

www.ingramcontent.com/pod-product-compliance
Lightning Source LLC
LaVergne TN
LVHW052314200926
848481LV00002B/565